The Mughal Empire

A Captivating Guide to the Mughal Empire in South Asia and the Impact the Mughals Had on the History of India

Free Bonus from Captivating History (Available for a Limited time)

Hi History Lovers!

Now you have a chance to join our exclusive history list so you can get your first history ebook for free as well as discounts and a potential to get more history books for free! Simply visit the link below to join.

Captivatinghistory.com/ebook

Also, make sure to follow us on Facebook, Twitter and Youtube by searching for Captivating History.

Contents

Introduction

The Mughal Empire, also known as the Moghul Empire, lasted for about three centuries, and at its peak, it covered 3.2 million square kilometers, from the outer borders of the Indus Basin in the west to the highlands of Assam and Bangladesh in the east, and from Afghanistan and Kashmir in the north to the Deccan Plateau in the south. The Mughal Empire also took the territories of what used to be known as Hindustan in the northern Indian subcontinent. With such a large territory came many diverse peoples, roughly numbering 150 million souls. The name "Mughal" comes from the Persian word for Mongols, which, over time, came to mean only the Islamic people of Babur's dynasty in India.

During its peak, the Mughal Empire was one of humanity's most powerful and richest political entities, overshadowed maybe only by contemporary China. The empire relied on its military, and as such, most of its income was spent on supplying and maintaining the most modern army of the period. The rulers relied on conquest, which would reward the most loyal soldiers and bring new lands and people who would farm it. The Mughal Empire mostly owes the success of its army to its visionary founders, who employed foreign gunpowder experts that helped to bring destruction upon their enemies. The power of the early Mughal Empire was unmatched in the whole of

India, and once the father of the empire, Babur, started conquering the lands, there was no stopping them.

The origins of the Mughal Empire can be found in the Muslim territories of Central Asia, and even though they were not the first Islamic rulers of northern India, they were certainly newcomers who had to adapt and overcome additional difficulties compared to the native rulers. Even though the land was rich with people and fertile grounds, it was completely new to Babur and his Central Asian warriors. As foreigners, they had to face many uprisings from the domesticated Muslims and Hindus, who defied bowing to rulers coming from distant lands. It took generations for the Mughals to settle in their new lands and take full control over the diverse peoples that eventually became their new subjects.

The Mughals, as well as the Mongols, whom the Mughals originated from, were considered to be uncultured yet fierce warriors. During their three-century rule in northern India, the Mughals transformed from a warrior tribe to one of the most sophisticated empires, developing court etiquettes and promoting the fine arts. The empire turned from fierce conquerors to becoming the center of the Indian world, and many people came here for education or to practice their crafts. The Mughal Empire was never an indigenous national empire, and it never had a mono-ethnic army. The Mughals were always diverse peoples who found a way to coexist with other cultures in very demanding times.

However, the Mughal Empire continued expanding to the point where it could only break. The administration eventually failed, with uprisings destroying the fringes of the empire, and it began its downfall, which would last for one and a half centuries. In the end, it was led by a series of weak rulers who were unable to hold the empire together. Like sand running through their fingers, the empire was lost bit by bit. Both Indian and European challengers dismantled it completely, leaving only the city of Old Delhi as a remembrance of the once glorious empire. Finally, in 1857, the Mughal Empire was no more, and the descendants of a once royal dynasty were dispersed through the Indian subcontinent, living the lives of commoners.

Chapter 1 – Origins of the Mughal Empire

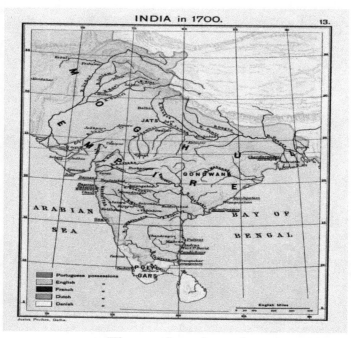

The empire at its peak
https://en.wikipedia.org/wiki/Mughal_Empire#/media/
File:Joppen1907India1700a.jpg

On March 4th, 1519, the son of martial adventurer and ruler of Kabul Babur, was born. He was named Hindal, Taker of India, since Hindal was born in the same year Babur requested the submission of Ibrahim, the young sultan of Delhi. To persuade Ibrahim to submit, Babur sent him gifts and an ultimatum. But those didn't work on the young sultan, whose family had ruled northern India for generations in a territory known as Hindustan. Babur claimed the right to rule northern India because his ancestor, Timur, had conquered Delhi a century earlier. But those Indians who were familiar with the name of Timur, few as they were, were weary as they had only heard the stories of his raids and the devastation he brought to the land.

Ibrahim's governor in Lahore denied access to Babur and his small war party, and he didn't even bother to notify the sultan of his arrival. In his memoirs, known as the *Baburnama*, Babur complained that the people of Hindustan had no wisdom as they didn't dare to stand against their enemies, nor did they know how to respond to the act of friendship. Thus declined, this Central Asian martial adventurer could only return home to enjoy his newborn son. However, seven years later, he would invade Hindustan and kill the young Sultan Ibrahim. With this conquest, Babur came to possess the royal treasuries of the former sultanate, which were rich enough to give him power over the whole region. The Mughal Empire was thus born.

Babur (r. 1526–1530)

Babur, the first emperor of the Mughal Empire
https://en.wikipedia.org/wiki/Babur#/media/File:Babur_of_India.jpg

Babur's true name was Zahir-ud-Din, which means "Defender of Faith" in Arabic. His date of birth was recorded as being on February 14th, 1483, in Andijan, which is in today's Uzbekistan. On his father's side, he was a descendant of Timur of the Timurid Empire. On his mother's side, he was a direct descendant of Genghis Khan of the Mongol Empire. With ancestors like that, it is no wonder Babur strived to rule his whole life. He was the eldest son of the ruler of the Fergana Valley, Umar Shaikh Mirza II of the Barlas tribe. The title of mirza was often used by the leaders of various Persian tribes, such as Babur's father, but later, it would transform, and only the princes of the royal family of the Mughals would be honored with the title, as well as some distinguished military commanders. The Barlas tribe was of Mongolian origin, but they did embrace Turkic and Persian culture as their identity and Islam as their faith. Scholars believe that because of this mixture of cultures, specifically Mongolian and Arabic, Babur was able to gain the support of many people from Central Asia, especially Iranians and those of Turkic origin. His army was ethnically diverse as it included Persians, Arabs, Afghans, Barlas, and other Turko-Mongol tribes of Central Asia. It is believed that his true name, Zahir-ud-Din, was too complicated to pronounce for his multiethnic army and that it was them who gave him the nickname Babur, a Persian word that means "tiger."

In 1494, when he was only eleven years old, Babur's father died. However, even at that young age as a ruler, Babur managed to secure his rightful place as the leader of the Fergana Valley. However, his position was threatened by his own uncles, and they weren't the only ones who threatened the boy's position. A part of the people he now ruled believed that his younger brother, Jahangir, would be a more formidable leader. It is important to understand that the Central Asian peoples did not follow the usual primogeniture laws of inheritance, where the rule is passed from the father to his eldest son. As long as the male child was recognized as legitimate, he had the right to inherit the rule. As such, it wasn't unusual in Central Asia to see brothers at war with each other. Babur had the help of his grandmother, Aisan Daulat Begum. She was his mother's mother and the first wife of Yunus Khan of Moghulistan. All of this contributed to a dynastic turmoil, which was common within the ruling families. As warrior peoples, these clans were constantly at conflict, and after the passing of Babur's father, they saw an opportunity to gain new territories.

This is this cultural setting in which Babur grew up in, and when he was fifteen, he planned his first military conquest. He wanted to conquer Samarkand, a city that lay in the Bukhara region. For the next seven months, his army besieged the city. The losses were heavy on both sides, but Babur managed to gain the submission of the neighboring forts. While moving his army from one position to the other, the citizens of Samarkand wrongly thought he was retreating, and they decided to attack. They sent their soldiers outside of the city, and Babur had the opportunity to confront them on the open field. Finally, he was able to show off his military power, and his cavalry overran the army of Samarkand.

However, the city still endured, and winter was fast approaching. Unwilling to leave the territory, Babur decided to spend the winter with his army in one of the forts that submitted to him. This pause of the siege allowed Baysonqor Mirza, the sultan of Bukhara, to ask

Muhammad Shaybani, an Uzbek warrior, for help. He led his army of around three thousand men to Samarkand, where he met Babur for the first time—Shaybani would later become a true nemesis of Babur. However, disappointed by the cold reception he encountered in the city of Samarkand, Shaybani left after only a few days.

Seeing that his last hope, the Uzbek army, was gone, Baysonqor Mirza abandoned the city and his kingdom. With a small retinue of followers, he left for Afghanistan. When their leader left, the citizens of Samarkand had no other choice than to surrender to the one who had besieged them, and Babur finally took the city without any opposition. Samarkand used to be the capital of Emperor Timur, and in the 16th century, it continued to be one of the biggest, richest, and most respected cities. And now, fifteen-year-old Babur ruled it.

However, the long siege cost the city, and there was not enough plunder for Babur's army, so many soldiers deserted due to lack of payment. There was not enough food for the citizens either, and the fertile fields outside of the city weren't plowed. Farmers had no seeds to plant, making the upcoming harvest difficult. As if the troubles in Samarkand weren't enough, back home in the Fergana Valley, the nobles who supported his brother rebelled, and Jahangir Mirza was proclaimed the new king. With the few troops he was left with, Babur marched to reclaim his kingdom. But since the troops were dissatisfied, they eventually left him. Babur was now without an army, without Samarkand, and without his kingdom.

So, for the next three years, Babur gathered an army. He recruited troops from all the ethnicities of Central Asia. Finally, once his army was strong enough, he launched another attack on Samarkand. And his siege was successful, as he managed to take and rule it for almost one hundred days.

But his rival Muhammad Shaybani was back with no intention to leave. This time, he wanted to conquer the city for himself, not for a sultan who treated him as an inferior. During the three years that Babur had spent gathering his army, Shaybani led a series of successful campaigns with which he gained power among the Uzbeks.

In 1500/01, Babur had to negotiate for peace. The situation was indeed very bad as he not only had to offer his sister Khanzada Begum's hand in marriage to Muhammad Shaybani, but he also had to leave the city. Babur had nowhere to go, so he decided to try and take his old kingdom back, the Fergana Valley. But his army, already tired and decimated by the fighting at Samarkand, stood no chance to win back Fergana. In fact, Babur lost everything but his life. With a small group of warriors, he escaped and tried to find his luck in Tashkent, a city ruled by one of his uncles. However, he wasn't welcomed there, and he wrote in his memoirs how he was often humiliated by his uncle and his court. He lived in poverty, and he only survived due to the compassion of his friends and strangers. Only ten years after gaining control over Fergana, Babur was now a prince in exile.

One of Babur's paternal uncles ruled Kabul, but he died in 1501, leaving an opportunity for the prince in exile to reclaim his throne, as the only heir of Kabul was just an infant. However, a rivaling Timurid prince was quicker in seizing the city, marrying the daughter of the previous ruler to make his conquest legitimate. But that didn't help, as he was still seen as a usurper, and the people he ruled resented him. When Babur gathered an army of 200 loyal followers, the people of Kabul welcomed him as a savior. After all, he was the nephew to their previous ruler, which gave him all the legitimacy he needed. With ease, Babur dispatched the usurper and started ruling his newly gained kingdom.

In 1506, Babur allied himself with his cousin, Sultan Husayn Mirza Bayqara of Herat, and their intention was to attack Muhammad Shaybani together. However, Bayqara died the same year, and his sons didn't want to go to war. Babur stayed in Herat for the next two months, as it was the capital of eastern Muslim culture at the time. There, he learned about history and language, which inspired him to start writing his memoirs. After Babur left, the city of Herat was conquered by Shaybani, and Bayqara's sons were killed. Babur was now the most powerful ruler of the Timurid dynasty, and as such, he started calling himself Padshah, meaning the "Great King" or "Emperor." Many relatives and princes of the neighboring regions sought shelter in Kabul, as Shaybani ravaged their lands. The ancestral lands of the Timurid dynasty were now all conquered by the Uzbek leader Shaybani, who became a real threat to Kabul.

Some princes and nobles of Kabul didn't believe Babur would be able to protect them from the attacks of the Uzbeks, and they organized a rebellion. However, Babur was able to quell it pretty quickly. Two years later, though, another rebellion started, and this time, the military generals of Kabul managed to expel Babur. However, Babur still had loyal friends in the city who advocated for him, and the leaders of the rebels switched to his side, allowing Babur to take over the city once more.

In the meantime, Shaybani was killed in 1510 during the conflict he had with Ismail I, the shah of Shia Safavid Persia. Uzbek power was diminishing, and Babur allied himself with Shah Ismail to regain his ancestral territories of Central Asia. In 1513, he left for Samarkand to lay siege to it for the third time. There, he was reunited with his sister, who had been forced to marry Babur's enemy Shaybani. Babur ruled Samarkand for the next three years, but in 1514, he returned to Kabul after he lost Samarkand to the Uzbeks for the third time.

Babur spent the next eleven years ruling in relative peace. He took the time to reorganize his army in preparation for the conquest of Hindustan, and he carried out small raids in the territory of northern India and successfully dealt with small rebellions in the area of modern Afghanistan. Even though the regions were relatively peaceful, Babur undertook the long and demanding task of modernizing his army.

Formation of the Empire

The Uzbeks remained a threat, and as Babur records in his memoirs, he wanted to put some space between his people and their enemies. Although some of his people found refuge in Badakhshan, just north of Kabul, Babur looked to India, as it was a much farther and safer place. Since Babur had lost Samarkand, he chose to dedicate himself to conquering the territories of India. As a first step, he started reorganizing his fractured army. In 1519, he was ready to embark on his first campaign to today's Pakistan. Following the footsteps of his predecessor Timur, Babur wanted to spread his influence to Punjab, as these regions used to be a part of the Timurid Empire.

At this time, parts of northern India were ruled by Sultan Ibrahim of the Lodi dynasty. However, Ibrahim's rule was weak, and his empire deteriorated. Many of the followers of the Indian sultan decided to switch sides and join Babur. It was at this point that Babur sent an ambassador with gifts to the young sultan asking him to recognize Babur as his supreme ruler. However, the ambassador was detained in Lahore and didn't even see the sultan. Instead, he spent many months as a prisoner.

In 1524, Babur started his main campaign to take over Punjab, but he was met there by the forces of Ibrahim Lodi, which had disposed of his uncle, Daulat Khan Lodi, the ruler of Punjab. In Lahore, the armies met, and the Lodi army was forced to retreat, but Babur wasn't satisfied by this turn of events. Instead, he burned the city for the next two days and then installed Alam Khan, another rebellious uncle of Ibrahim Lodi, as the governor. Alam lost the city once Babur left with his army, and he had to run to Kabul. There, he was met by Babur's army, who helped him reach his brother, Daulat Khan Lodi. Together, Ibrahim's uncles besieged Delhi. However, the young sultan easily defeated the united army, and Babur realized that Punjab would be much harder to conquer then he initially thought.

During the year 1525, Babur was staying in Peshawar, a trade center on the route between India and Central Asia. There, he received news that Daulat Khan Lodi had abandoned him and joined his nephew, Sultan Ibrahim. Babur decided to confront Daulat Khan, and he marched his troops to what is known to history as the First Battle of Panipat. After Babur crossed the Indus River in November 1526 and entered Punjab with his mighty army, Daulat Khan surrendered without a fight as his army abandoned him upon seeing the force of Babur. Daulat Khan was pardoned once he granted the rule over Punjab to Babur. The army continued on, and on April 20th, 1526, they reached Panipat, which was only 90 kilometers (almost 56 miles) away from Delhi, where the army of Sultan Ibrahim Lodi was waiting.

Babur records that Ibrahim's army was superior. It numbered 100,000 soldiers and 100 elephants against Babur's 15,000 men. But the numbers didn't deter Babur; instead, he devised a plan. He used the city of Panipat as protection for his right flank. A trench was also dug out and covered with branches to hide it to serve as a defense for the left flank of the army. In the center, between the city and the trench, Babur placed 700 carts that were tied together with ropes, and they served as a defense for the artillery. This was essential to protect, as his modernized army relied on the use of gunpowder, as he employed Turkish cannon specialists and had created the matchlock infantry. Babur's army was placed between the city and the trench, and those defenses created a narrow approach for Ibrahim's soldiers.

The sultan was forced to reorganize his army, as he had hoped for an open field battle. Babur took the opportunity of Ibrahim's confusion to deploy a tactic known as *tulughma*, in which he split his army into smaller units and created front and rear flanks. Because his army was much smaller than Ibrahim's, his only chance was to surround the enemy from all sides. Ibrahim relied heavily on his elephants and cavalry, but Babur had modernized his army and used cannons against them. Two flanks, a side and a rear, attacked Lodi's army, massacring them. Both sides suffered heavy losses, but Babur was able to win the battle in just three hours against a much stronger enemy by using a mixture of Ottoman and Mongolian tactics. Sultan Ibrahim Lodi was killed during the battle, and thus, the Delhi Sultanate ceased to exist.

Babur was now the ruler of northern India, and by taking the territories that used to belong to the Lodi dynasty, he set the foundations for his future Mughal Empire. But he was challenged by neighboring magnates who wanted to take advantage of the opportunity of regional instability and take Lodi's throne for themselves. Before setting in motion the construction of his empire, he had to defeat these new challengers, especially one named Rana Sanga, the ruler of Mewar. Rana is the title used only by absolute Hindu monarchs. It is equivalent to an emperor, unlike raja, which is equivalent to a king. In this context, the title of maharaja can be translated as "high king" and was also used like the European title "the Great," such as Alexander the Great or Alfred the Great. The two armies met at the Battle of Khanwa on March 17th, 1527.

Rana Sanga recognized the strength of his enemy Babur, and to fight him, he allied with all the kings of Rajasthan, a state of northern India, who either joined the battle personally or sent a contingent of soldiers. The alliance also included Mahmud Lodi, the younger brother of Ibrahim Lodi. He was proclaimed the sultan of the Afghans shortly after his brother's death, and he brought 10,000 of his soldiers to the battle. Hasan Khan Mewati, the ruler of Mewat, brought 12,000 soldiers. Others who joined the army were rulers of the various cities of Rajasthan, including Harauti, Dungarpur, Dhundhar, Jalor, and Sirohi. The Rajput-Afghan alliance had a mission of expelling Babur, who was seen as a Turkic intruder from the Lodi empire.

Babur's memoirs record Rana Sanga's army numbering 200,000 men. However, historians consider this number to be an exaggeration and believe that the Rajput army had only 40,000 soldiers. However, this exaggeration most likely means that the alliance had a much larger army than Babur, no matter what the real numbers were. As Babur's army was outnumbered once more, his men suffered from low morale, and to raise it, Babur gave a religious meaning to the battle. He proclaimed that he would live in total abstinence from wine from that day forward. He even broke all his drinking cups and spilled all the liquor on the ground to show his intentions were sincere. His actions not only impacted his army but his enemies as well.

The battle took place on March 16th, 1527, near Khanwa in the Agra District of Uttar Pradesh. Babur reused the tactics from the previous battle in Panipat, as he used carts to create a defense for his artillery. His matchlock infantry hid behind wheeled shields made out of rawhide stretched on tripods. This way, they would have protection, and they could easily advance or retreat. With further modernization of his army, Babur had no difficulty defeating his enemy, who fought in the traditional way. Yet again, he surrounded the enemy army and ordered his artillery and matchlocks to advance. The carts, which protected the artillery, were pushed forward, and the cannons followed. The allied army of Rana Sanga fought hard, but Raja Shiladitya of northeastern Malwa deserted and took his soldiers to Babur's side. Rana was defeated, and to show his disrespect toward his enemy, Babur ordered a tower of enemy skulls to be built. These towers were common Ottoman tactics of frightening their adversaries, but they also served as memorials to the battles.

Rana Sanga escaped the battlefield alive, and he found refuge in Chittor, but the alliance he built collapsed after this battle, never again to be united against their common enemy. Scholars comment that Rana Sanga would have probably defeated Babur if there were no cannons in Babur's artillery, as Rana held the superiority in numbers, not to mention the famous bravery of the Rajput soldiers. Rana died the next year, in late January 1528, in Chittor. He wanted to confront Babur once more, but his generals considered such a move to be suicide. Instead of openly opposing him, they decided to poison him.

However, the word that Rana planned to renew the conflict reached Babur, and he decided to attack one of the allied forces, Medini Rai, the ruler of eastern Malwa. He hoped that by defeating the allies of Rana Sanga, he would be able to isolate Rana Sanga and deal with him easily. So, Babur marched his army to Chanderi in January of 1528, which fell after just two days. To avoid capture and enslavement, the women and children of Chanderi committed the ritual of Jauhar, a self-immolation ceremony.

Chapter 2 – In the New Land

Difficulties of the New Empire

Babur founded the Mughal Empire for his Central Asian followers. However, they were all new to the region and found themselves ruling over people who spoke different languages and had different cultures, religions, and values. Babur was an alien to the Hindustan he now ruled, and his new subjects did not speak Persian or the Turkic language of Babur's followers. Not even the Afghans who inhabited this part of the world spoke these languages. As a foreign emperor, Babur was an intruder in the eyes of the people of Hindustan. They regarded him as an illegitimate ruler who had invaded them. Because of it, Babur had to rely on his military power to rule over his new subjects.

In order to maintain his expensive army, Babur had to reward the commanders and pay the soldiers. But since his empire was new, he didn't have a proper land taxation system. To finance his army, Babur had to capture the royal treasures of neighboring cities. However, this meant the constant expansion of his empire, for which he had no resources. Each year, he had to launch campaigns in the neighboring provinces, which, one by one, submitted to his rule, from the east where the Sultanate of Bengal ruled to the west where the nomadic rulers of the Baloch people lived. All these conquered peoples agreed to pay a yearly tribute to Babur, but only while they were under immediate threat. As soon as the Mughal army retreated, they would stop sending money, treasures, food, and other resources.

The cities that resisted the longest were always given to Babur's Central Asian commanders. These cities were extorted, as they had to pay for the army's maintenance, including their pleasures, but they also had to send a yearly tribute to Babur's personal treasury. However, the commanders who ruled these cities were strangers, and they often had a hard time finding a common language with the locals, who took every opportunity to disobey their invaders. Commanders were often too frightened to take up residency inside the city, choosing to set up their quarters in the military garrisons outside the city walls instead. In addition, Babur would often recall his commanders when he needed them for new military campaigns, and there was no one left to gather the tribute from these cities. Babur would also relocate his commanders too often, which wouldn't allow the commanders to make any kind of bond with the locals and convince them of the intentions for the newly formed empire.

Babur's army was modernized with guns and cannons. Thus, it was a very expensive army to maintain. It was this modernization and use of gunpowder that allowed Babur to successfully capture Hindustan, as his opponents fought in the traditional way without access to gunpowder and new military technologies. Babur was employing Ottoman gunpowder experts, the most prominent among them being Master Ustad Ali Quli and Mustafa Rumi Khan. Both of them came from Constantinople or what Central Asians called *Rumi*, meaning second Rome. This is why Mustafa's title was "Rumi Khan," to indicate his importance. This title would later be given to other artillery commanders who distinguished themselves in Babur's military campaigns.

The cannons Babur paid so expensively for were indeed powerful, and they helped immensely in conquering Hindustan. However, they had some limitations. They were long-ranged weapons, perfect for use when the target was across a river or stationed within a citadel. But they did not have enough power to breach the walls of large cities unless the cannons were positioned on higher ground. Also, the cannons needed a long cooling time in between shots, as the barrel could easily crack if overheated. The maximum number of shots of Babur's cannons was sixteen per day. It wasn't that bad of a number considering how powerful they were. But, on the other hand, they weren't reliable. The mortar would shatter and wound or even kill his own soldiers. The cannons were also very large, and they needed to be pulled by elephants. Babur had to cut down whole jungles to make roads for the transportation of these cannons, which was mostly considered to be a major time-waster.

The cavalry and infantry of Babur's army were the most easily maintained. Cavalry was often rewarded with local lands, which their families could live and work on. Infantry was easily dismissed and called back to service. But the gunpowder experts had to stay in Babur's employment, and he had to finance them regularly, often from his own treasuries. Because of the number of valuable soldiers who wielded muskets and cannons, Babur emptied Sultan Ibrahim's treasuries after only two years of ruling his new Mughal Empire. The commanders he assigned as governors of the conquered cities were pressed to send him more and more revenue, which further created mistrust from the local populace.

The people of Hindustan weren't the only problems Babur's new empire encountered. The environment of northern India wasn't the same as in their homelands in Central Asia. The extreme temperatures and the rainfall variations of the monsoon seasons were all new to Babur's followers. Even though the heartland of the Mughal Empire was all fertile land, they lacked rain during the whole year. And the outskirts of the empire in Rajasthan and the Indus plains were close to the environment of a desert. The Central Asians were used to drylands; however, they weren't prepared for the high temperatures of India. In the winter, the monsoon season would hit the northern parts of India once more, making it possible for the Mughals in the heartland to have a second harvest, but the other parts of the empire would experience drought and a lack of food. Since Babur was relying on military campaigns to finance his empire, the land was often at war, and the transportation of food to the hunger-stricken areas was often disrupted.

Religion and Culture

Babur didn't have enough Central Asian commanders who he could employ as governors or in other positions of his administration. So, he began to recruit Indians for his army and court, but they would only be given commanding posts and higher offices if they were Muslims. Most of the recruits were Shaikhzadas, Indians whose ancestors had converted to Islam much earlier. Northern India was also home to many Afghans who had settled there a few centuries earlier, and they were also welcomed in the ranks of Babur's army and court.

Non-Muslims were either given positions of subordinate officers, common soldiers, workers, or scribes. Some of them even previously served Sultan Ibrahim, but Babur needed them, as they were experienced and well-informed. They were also valuable workers, as they were natives, and their roots were from the land he now ruled. They were a source of information for Babur, as they knew the revenues each city was paying to Ibrahim and what could potentially be exploited from the new regions his army would conquer. Because Babur started employing Hindu scribes and administrative workers, his court was attractive enough for thousands of Indian artists, masons, and servants to flock to his empire, who found employment at his court or in the households of his
commanders.

Babur was spiritually tied to Sufism, a form of Islamic mysticism that followed the precepts set by the prophet Muhammad. More correctly, he belonged to the Naqshbandi order, just like his ancestor Timur. The Naqshbandi traced its spiritual lineage to Muhammad through his father-in-law, Abu Bakr, unlike other orders that do it through the prophet's close relatives. It was the principles of this Islamic order that Babur set as the main spiritual support of his whole regime. Any member of the Naqshbandi was a prominent courtier of Emperor Babur. His devotion to the order is probably best displayed through his vow to versify *Risala-i Walidiyya*, which was written by Pir Khwaja, a long-dead Naqshbandi Sufi master. The poem had 243 lines, and Babur even claimed that it was these verses that helped him overcome his constant desire for wine.

However, as the emperor of the Mughals, Babur started honoring the India-based Sufi masters, such as the Shattari or Suhrawardi pirs. To clarify, the word pir, in the context of Islam, is used as a title for spiritual leaders. Sultan Ibrahim granted revenues to the religious institutions that honored these pirs, and when Babur started his rule over the northern Indian territories, he renewed the revenue streams. He often invested in other Sufi orders that had a wide network of religious institutions across India. By doing so, Babur reinforced the legitimacy of his rule, and he ensured that religious leaders would support his descendants. However, many of the pirs fought each other for religious and political supremacy, and they vied for Babur's financial support.

Through Babur's memoirs, there is a strong sense of the ambivalence about settling in Hindustan. Even so, he remained open-minded toward all the new experiences India brought to him and his Central Asian followers. He was particularly fascinated by the diversity of nature and animal life in India, as well as the artistry of Indian masons and monuments. In his autobiography, Babur explained in detail the measurement systems used across India, but he never paid enough attention to its peoples and their cultures. However, he did express his shock that Indian peasants, both male and female, went around half-naked due to the heat of the regions. He also couldn't grasp the artistic value of India's nude sculptures, and a large number of these were destroyed on his orders. Some scholars believe Babur was too prude and that he was not motivated by religion when he ordered the destruction of the nude statues in Gwalior.

Though he might have been prude, he didn't shy away from the pleasurable places he discovered or built himself. He was famous for building many gardens in the Central Asian style, which would shelter him and his followers from the discomfort of India. He was always bothered by the hot, dry air and dust in some of the regions of his empire, and he was in a constant search for suitable places where he could build pleasure refuges. Since his court was nomadic, Babur's whole household would move from one region to another. Because of that, he needed a network of walled residences with these elaborate gardens that would protect him from the elements of the Indian subcontinent. In his *Baburnama*, he described his shock at the low cost of Indian masons and artisans, whom he employed to build these gardens. He also complimented their skill and their numbers, but he never named one individual. Babur always referred to them in the plural and by their profession. Because he was constantly closed behind walls with his Central Asian commanders, he created even more distance between himself and the locals. This is why his walled residences were nicknamed "Kabul" by the Indian populace, who had nothing in common with their ruler.

Babur's Mughal Empire was a vast territory. As such, it was rich in culture, but it was also rich in gold and silver. Babur displayed mixed feelings about living in Hindustan. He was attracted to its riches, but he hated its climate. In his writings, he even admits he was seduced by the wealth India brought but that he hated the land. Although he would sometimes display enjoyment in what India had to offer, he often longed for the more pleasing climate of Central Asia.

Succession and the End of the Life of Babur

Babur ruled his Mughal Empire for only four years. In Hindustan, his health constantly declined. At one point, because of his fragile health, some noblemen conspired against his sons for the succession. They wanted to install another nobleman, who was also a descendant of Timur, as the ruler of the Mughals. His name was Mir Muhammad Mahdi Khwaja, and he was the new husband of Babur's sister Khanzada Begum. However, since the empire he created was a patrimonial state, his commanders agreed to his wishes of succession.

Babur's sons all became deputies during Babur's life, and he was aware that once he would die, his sons would become each other's rival. To prevent this from happening, he started distributing his territories among the four sons he had. He already installed Kamran, his second son, as the ruler of Kabul in his absence, and Babur wanted Kamran to hold Kabul even after his death. To the eldest son, Humayun, he planned to leave Hindustan. His youngest sons, Hindal and Askari, were to be given territories in Kabul. In his will, Babur directed his sons to respect each other and to support one another, as it was the principle of Central Asian sovereignty.

However, the distrust and rivalry between the brothers were obvious even during Babur's life. When he was ill in 1529, Babur summoned his younger son, Hindal, to his side, but his eldest, Humayun, ordered his brother to stay in Badakhshan and rule instead of him while he visited their ill father. When Babur heard of this, he sent an invitation to Hindal once more, and as the supreme emperor, he overruled Humayun's order. He was very displeased with his eldest son, as he was too willful. But Gulbadan, one of Babur's daughters who wrote the biography of Humayun (*Humayun-Nama*), records her father's fondness for his eldest son. She recalls his love was so great that when Humayun was sick, Babur performed a ritual to transfer the sickness to himself. Humayun recovered while his father began to die. He spent his final days in Agra, which was where he died in 1530. At first, he was buried there, but later, his body was transported to Kabul, which was where he wished to be laid to rest.

Despite Babur's will and the division of his territories, his sons fought for supremacy continuously. Humayun was the successor to the Mughal Empire, but he ultimately proved to be unable to maintain control.

Chapter 3 – Humayun of the Mughal Empire

Humayun, the second emperor
https://en.wikipedia.org/wiki/Humayun#/media/File:Darbar_of_Humayun,
_detail,_Humayun._Akbarnama,_1602-4,_British_Library.png

When Babur died in 1530, he was succeeded by his eldest son, Humayun. The young prince was unfamiliar with the lands he inherited, as most of his time was spent outside of India. He had returned to Central Asia after having spent a year fighting his father's wars for conquest in 1526. He only returned to India after he received the news of his father's illness, shortly before he died.

Upon his succession of the Mughal throne, Humayun faced a revolt led by his own brothers. Each of them had their own dynastic ambitions, and they claimed independence from their older brother's rule. Mirza Kamran ruled Kabul, as was his father's wish. However, soon after Babur's death, he expanded his dominion over Kandahar, parts of Central Asia, and Punjab. The main rivalry among brothers was between Humayun and Kamran, while the younger ones, Hindal and Askari, switched their loyalty between them as they pleased. On some occasions, they claimed independence for the regions they controlled. It came to the point where Kamran's forces killed his younger brother Hindal, and an angered Humayun ordered him and Askari to be exiled.

The four brothers also had a cousin, who Babur had adopted as a son, named Mirza Sulaiman. He ruled Badakhshan after Babur's death, and he also accepted the overlordship of Humayun and Kamran, depending on where the political power at the given moment was. He also asserted autonomy for his regions against the will of Babur's sons. While Humayun, Kamran, Hindal, and Askari died fighting each other, Sulaiman outlived them all.

Humayun inherited a large empire, and to effectively control it, he needed to be familiar with the policies and techniques of ruling. Unfortunately, the young prince wasn't. Instead, he sought to install himself as a divine symbol of power, and he organized his court in the image of the cosmic order as it was seen by 16th-century Islam. He thought of himself as the center of the microcosmos that was his court. He was divine, and as such, he wore a veil over his face, sheltering it from the curious courtiers who wanted to bask in his divine splendor. He would occasionally lift his veil and allow his subjects to be dazzled by the light of his image. Personally, he was a follower of the Shattari Sufi mysticism order, which sought to control the cosmic forces through the practice of yoga. It was Humayun who ordered all of his royal tents to be divided into twelve parts, with each part representing one of the zodiac signs. Also, he named the days of the week by celestial bodies and dressed ritually according to what day it was. For example, Tuesday was Mars Day, and he would dress in red robes to symbolically represent the celestial body. Also, he devoted Tuesday to sentencing criminals and war prisoners.

Humayun believed that his imaginative ritualistic rule would persuade his brothers about his supremacy. He divided the administration of the empire according to the natural elements. The military was fire, while the land and building administration was earth. The irrigation of the empire was entrusted to the ministry of water, while his own household was administered by the element of air. Each state official had to wear a robe in the color that belonged to the element of his ministry. The military wore red, land and buildings wore brown robes, the water ministry wore blue, and the royal household was dressed in white. But all of these efforts of symbolism failed to impress his rival brothers, his Central Asian followers, and his new subjects, whether they were Muslim or not. His Central Asian commanders, in particular, resisted his effort to centralize the power in his own persona. They wanted the old ways where they were given positions in the governance, and Humayun had to face repeated uprisings due to his policies.

Early Military Successes

Even though Humayun wasn't familiar with his new Mughal Empire, upon succeeding the throne, he decided to conquer as much of South Asia as possible. He wanted to continue his father's military momentum even though he was surrounded by very rich and powerful rulers and warlords. The Central and Lower Ganges Plains had an ever-shifting coalition of Indo-Afghans and the Sultanate of Bengal. The coalition was supported by local magnates and landowners. Against them, Humayun had some initial victories, but the real threat came from the southwest, where Sultan Bahadur Shah of Gujarat ruled.

Bahadur Shah sought Babur's help when he was fleeing the wrath of his own father and older brother during the dynastic struggle in the

Gujarat region. But Babur denied him any help, and he described Bahadur Shah in his writings as a bloodthirsty and audacious man. Nevertheless, Bahadur managed to seize the throne of his father, putting him in charge of the main ports of India, which were crucial for the international trade across the Indian Ocean. Because of this, Bahadur was extremely wealthy, and he used his riches to secure the loyalties of other rulers in the region. He hired and maintained a large army, which he supplied with expensive artillery. He even had Mustafa Rumi Khan as a commander of his artillery forces, one of the gunpowder experts mentioned earlier.

Bahadur Shah was powerful enough to challenge Humayun, and he did so by attacking the Chittor Fort, which defended the point of access to Hindustan. The first attack on the fort was launched in 1533, but it was unsuccessful, and it was followed by a second attack in 1534. Humayun arrived too late to save the fortress, but he decided to invade and conquer his enemy's territory, Gujarat. The armies met at Malwa, where Sultan Bahadur Shah decided to entrench his army behind the fort walls, which were defended by cannons. However, Humayun's forces besieged the fort and starved the army, forcing it to flee. After seeing the defeat, Rumi Khan decided to switch to Humayun's side and join his efforts in conquering Gujarat. Bahadur Shah sought refuge with the governor of Portuguese India, Nuno da Cunha, who resided on the fortified island of Diu. However, Bahadur met his death on the island, as the negotiations with the governor didn't go well. He drowned, but it remains unclear if his death was an assassination or an accident as he was fleeing from the Portuguese.

While Humayun was on his military expedition to conquer the southwestern region of India, a rebellion rose in Hindustan, and his military commanders begged him to return home and deal with the rebels. But Humayun was convinced in his intentions to subdue the rich Gujarat territory, and he did not want to go back to Hindustan. His Central Asian generals then decided to support his younger half-brother, Askari, who was already in Agra, where he had proclaimed himself the sovereign. Humayun was forced to abandon his plans in

Gujarat, as he had to secure his power back in Hindustan. He managed to gain his throne back, and he even forgave his younger brother. But the military expenses were high, and since he had abandoned Gujarat, he had nothing to give in reward to his commanders. He needed loot in order to reward his supporters, who already showed how easily their loyalties could be lost. Humayun needed another military expedition urgently, and so, he marched his forces down the Ganges toward Bengal, where Indo-Afghan of the Sur clan, Sher Shah Suri, ruled. He was also known as Sher Khan, "Lion Lord."

Humayun's first major goal was to capture the Chunar fortress in 1537, which was placed in a strategically important geographical location in the region. The fortress was well defended by cannons on its walls, but Humayun's artillery prevailed after the four-month siege. Rumi Khan came up with the idea of placing the cannons on riverboats to bombard the fortress walls directly. They caused so much damage that Sher Shah's son, who commanded the fortress, agreed to negotiations. With the loss of Chunar, Sher Shah was forced to officially submit to the rule of Humayun. Because of his innovative tactics, Rumi Khan received this fortress as a reward. However, he was Indian, and as such, he stood out of the Central Asian circle of Humayun's commanders. He was assassinated by those commanders as soon as he fell into imperial disfavor.

Humayun's forces continued marching over Bengal in search of new treasures and rewards for the military. However, they were unaccustomed to the humidity of this area, and they suffered greatly. Even Humayun gave up the direct command of his forces and chose to close himself in his pleasure palace with his wives and concubines, enjoying opium. The situation back in Hindustan went sour once more when another of Humayun's half-brothers, this time Hindal, proclaimed himself to be the new ruler in Agra. Humayun had to go back and secure his throne once more, but it was the monsoon season, and the roads were impassable. Since Humayun had to delay his return to Hindustan, it created the opportunity for Sher Shah to reorganize his forces and block Humayun's return home.

The Loss of an Empire

It was in June 1539, as Humayun's forces were marching back to Hindustan, that Sher Shah met them once more at Chausa. This time, he had a more effective army, which managed to defeat the Mughal soldiers who were already dispirited by the harsh environment of Bengal. Humayun lost many of his Central Asian commanders, and one of his wives was killed, while the other one was captured. Humayun had to flee, and while crossing the river with his army, he nearly drowned. In his biography, it is recorded that a poor water-carrier named Nizam rescued the emperor. It also says that Nizam was rewarded by being named emperor for a day. However, this act enraged Humayun's commanders and courtiers, and they raised the question of his legitimacy to the throne. If he could transfer the sovereignty so freely, and to a man of low birth no less, what was so divine in him that demanded their respect? This disdain from his commanders continued to deepen as Humayun lost control over some of the Mughal territories. Furthermore, he was constantly challenged by his own brothers, and he had a bad opium habit that led him to resign from active rule from time to time. It is no wonder that Humayun's support was lessening each day.

In 1540, Humayun was resolved to return his lost prestige, and he decided to attack Sher Shah again. However, he lost once more, this time in the Battle of Bilgram on May 17th, 1540. The records note that his army was so demoralized that it scattered even before the main battle began. Humayun, with the help of an Afghan soldier, managed to escape. He decided to lavishly reward this soldier and admit him into the royal household, which created an even deeper divide between him and his commanders. This Afghan soldier, Shamsuddin Muhammad Atgah Khan, would later become Humayun's son's foster-father. Sher Shah drove Humayun out of Hindustan, and with the loss of the supporters in his own empire, Humayun had to search for refuge in Punjab. After only fourteen years, the Mughal Empire had ended. Sher Shah ruled in place of Humayun, but he did not rule as a Mughal emperor. Instead, he created his own dynasty in northern India, and the territory that was previously known as the Mughal Empire now became the Sur Empire.

Sher Shah ruled for seven years, from 1538 to 1545, and as a leader, he set up a new administration. Even though he ruled the area of Hindustan, Sher Shah chose Sasaram for his capital instead of Agra. Thee economic and military reorganization he implemented under his governance would further be used by the Mughals. Sher Shah contributed to the empire in so many ways that his Mughal successors would come to idolize him. He was the emperor who introduced the first *rupiya*, a silver coin whose name would later become a standard for the currency in the Indian subcontinent. He also organized the first Indian post office. Indeed, Sher Shah's accomplishments during his very short rule would be remembered forever. Even his nemesis Humayun referred to him as "Ustad-I-Badshahan," the teacher of kings.

However, not all was well within Sher Shah's empire. He was accused of leading religious persecutions, and his governance allowed religious violence across the provinces of northern India. He advised his own commanders that they should die during these religious persecutions and wars, for if they died while fighting against the infidels, they would become martyrs. His army oppressed the Hindus of India in particular. One such religious persecution took place at the Kalinjar fort, where every Hindu person—men, women, and children—was put to death. Sher Shah is also known for the destruction of many cities. In order to build a new city, he would destroy the historical site of the previous settlement and then build his city on its ruins. The city of Shergarh is the best example of this practice. This city used to be a site where Hinduism, Buddhism, and Jainism peacefully co-existed. The ruins of the previous settlement provide evidence of a thriving city's existence that preceded Sher Shah's rule.

Humayun the Exile

Humayun was still officially Padshah, and he sought some way to regain his empire. For that, he needed his place of exile to be strategically positioned for the reconquest of Hindustan. His brother Mirza Kamran held Kabul, but he wouldn't allow Humayun and his court passage to the Central Asian homeland. He thought of invading Kashmir, but his commanders were against it. Finally, he contemplated giving up on his empire and becoming a qalandar, a holy man of the Sufi order. In the end, a decision was made to move across the Thar Desert into Sindh, a province of modern Pakistan.

Humayun's court was constantly shrinking, as his Central Asian commanders who served under his father all left him. But he still had some riches, enough to be respected among some of his people but not enough to reward his supporters. In Sindh, some of the landowners were respectful enough to provide his small entourage with food, while others tried to drive him away from their lands. However, Humayun still had the loyalty of a Turkish warrior named Bairam Khan, whose family had been in the service of Babur. With his help and that of his soldiers, Humayun was able to extract enough provisions from those locals who weren't willing to part with their possessions.

According to his biography, which was written by his half-sister Gulbadan, Humayun was attracted to a daughter from a Persian family who was in his entourage. Her name was Hamida Begum, and she was in her early teens. She declined his marriage proposal, thinking she was not worthy of a man of such high status. Her father also objected as Humayun was too poor to marry at that time. But both her and her family eventually were persuaded, and a year after the wedding, in October of 1542, Hamida gave birth to a son named Akbar. A few months later, Humayun's entourage was attacked by his half-brother Askari, and he nearly captured Humayun. But he managed to escape, and together with Hamida and thirty of his faithful followers, he started the long march to Persia. However, his son Akbar was left behind and became his uncle's royal prisoner. A year later, Askari passed Akbar to Kamran, Humayun's brother, who ruled Kabul.

Humayun and his followers marched through mountains and valleys, and in these hostile areas, they were forced to kill their horses in order to eat their meat, which they cooked in soldiers' helmets. Humayun wrote a letter to Shah Tahmasp I of the Safavid dynasty about his coming to Persia. The letter was submissive and handwritten, a gesture that touched the court of Tahmasp so much that they welcomed Humayun and his followers with the greatest of honors. While visiting Persia, Humayun was amazed by its architecture and art, and later, he would employ Persian artists in his own court. The two rulers did not meet for the first six months of Humayun's stay in Persia. But once they did, many lavish parties were organized to celebrate the occasion. There is even a wall painting depicting the meeting of the two monarchs, and it still survives in Chehel Sotoun, Iran.

Shah Tahmasp treated the disgraced Mughal emperor with all the royal honors he could bestow, but he urged Humayun to convert from his Sunni beliefs to Shia Islam, which he accepted. His Mughal followers were reluctant to convert, but eventually, they agreed, as they saw that it was the only way in which Tahmasp would support Humayun's reconquest of the Mughal Empire. After he converted to Shia, Humayun proved to be of true value to Tahmasp. When Kamran offered Kandahar, located in today's Afghanistan, for the exchange of Humayun, Tahmasp refused him. In fact, the Persian ruler was so enraged that Kamran wanted Humayun dead that he prepared a great celebration, in which he announced he was giving Humayun 12,000 cavalrymen to attack Kamran. In return, he wanted to receive Kandahar from Humayun's own hands.

The Restoration of the Mughal Empire

Humayun started his mission to retake his empire in 1545, but it would take him over a decade to succeed. He started slowly by attacking Kandahar, where Askari ruled. With the help of Tahmasp's 12,000 cavalrymen, the city fell after being besieged for four weeks. As promised, he gave the city to Tahmasp, who appointed his infant son as its viceroy. However, the boy soon died, and Humayun thought himself strong enough to confront Tahmasp and rule the city by himself. But after some negotiations, the two monarchs agreed to install a governor who would rule the city under their joint sovereignty.

The same year, Humayun marched his army to take Kabul. Kamran Mirza wasn't loved by his people, and when his soldiers saw Humayun's Persian army approaching, they changed sides, numbering in the hundreds. Kabul was taken over with ease, and Humayun was reunited with his son, Akbar. They organized a large feast in the boy's honor. However, Kamran survived the onslaught, and he built a new army outside the city walls. He would cause Humayun to lose Kabul twice, but each time he did so, Humayun would manage to regain the city once more. Humayun thought of continuing and returning Hindustan under his rule, but he was aware the time wasn't right. Instead, he organized smaller raids, gaining more and more of his homeland territory back, which he would give as a reward to his commanders. This tactic attracted local warlords who offered their bands to Humayun's service. Thus, his army constantly grew.

Humayun suffered constant attacks from his brothers Kamran and Askari, who even captured his son Akbar on a few occasions. Each time he would forgive them until, in 1551, during a raid, they killed Hindal, who was, at the time, the subject of Humayun. To punish his brothers, Humayun exiled them both but not before blinding Kamran. With all of his three brothers out of his way, Humayun could concentrate on recovering Hindustan. He managed to recruit Persians and the younger generation of Central Asian warriors who didn't remember his own failures. In 1555, he took the opportunity of the existing dynastic struggle in the Sur Empire to launch his first attack. Briefly, Sher Shah had died ten years earlier when Humayun wasn't ready to attack. Sher Shah's successor, Islam Shah Suri, died in 1554, creating turmoil and rivalry among his three successors. All three Suri princes marched on Delhi to try and capture it, while the local leaders fought for their independence. The setting was perfect for a Mughal invasion.

Humayun placed his trust in Bairam Khan, a Turkish warlord who was a great tactician, and in February 1555, they captured Lahore and Rohtas Fort. After those conquests, his army took Dipalpur and Jalandhar in Punjab. Moving toward Delhi, where he planned to take the throne, Humayun and Bairam Khan met the Suri army, which numbered 30,000 men. The Mughal army easily defeated their enemy and occupied Sirhind. But Sikandar Shah Suri, one of the Suri pretenders to the throne, gathered an army of 80,000 soldiers and attacked Sirhind on June 22nd, 1555. However, Bairam Khan, the brilliant tactician, imitated the attack Sher Shah Suri had led against Humayun in the Battle of Chausa in 1539, and he defeated the Suri army once more. Humayun's path to Delhi was now open, and he quickly occupied the city, thus reestablishing the Mughal Empire.

Humayun decided to take a different approach to ruling his empire than before. Instead of a centralized state, he opted for the decentralization of the empire. He divided the empire into six semi-autonomous provinces that would be governed by different commanders. Humayun would be the paramount ruler to his new provinces of Delhi, Agra, Kanauj, Jaunpur, Mandu, and Lahore. He moved from province to province with his nomadic court and army, and he would supervise his governors and offer them his personal support when needed. Humayun's young son Akbar was sent to Lahore, where he would learn from Bairam Khan, whose task was to secure Punjab. Kabul was given to his second son, Mirza Muhammad Hakim, who was still an infant and needed the capable supervision of a trusted guardian.

Seven months after he restored the Mughal Empire, Humayun tripped while going down the steep stairs of his library, seriously injuring himself. Three days later, on January 27th, 1556, Humayun died from his injuries. It is said that Humayun had his arms full of books when he heard the call to prayer while descending the steps of the library. By habit, he bent his knee in a religious bow, but his foot caught his robe, and he tumbled down the steps, hitting his head on the edge of a stone.

Humayun was first buried inside a fort named Purana Quila, but his first wife, Bega Begum, commissioned a grand garden tomb in Delhi to be built in the Mughal style for her husband. This tomb was so grandiose that it set an example for the later Taj Mahal in Agra.

Chapter 4 – The Empire under Emperor Akbar

Akbar the Great
https://en.wikipedia.org/wiki/Akbar#/media/File:Govardhan._
Akbar_With_Lion_and_Calf_ca._1630,_Metmuseum_(cropped).jpg

Abu'l-Fath Jalal-ud-din Muhammad Akbar, better known as Akbar the Great, succeeded his father and ruled the Mughal Empire for nearly five decades, from 1556 until 1605. During his rule, the Mughal dynasty rooted itself in Hindustan. Unlike his grandfather and father, Akbar lived in Hindustan most of his life, as did his successors. He was born in Sindh, but he did spend a portion of his childhood in Central Asia as a royal prisoner in Kabul at the court of his uncle Kamran. However, Akbar was very young when his father died, and his accession did not go unchallenged.

To avoid the succession struggles, Humayun's advisors and courtiers held his death as a secret for several weeks. However, their actions did not help the underaged Akbar to strengthen his position as an emperor. He was under the regency of his father's greatest warrior Bairam Khan, and even though Bairam Khan tried to outmaneuver Akbar's rivals and dispatch a force that would defend the borders of the Mughal Empire against the successors of the Sur Empire, his Central Asian commanders didn't agree. In fact, many of them prepared to return to their homeland after Humayun's death.

At this time, back in Central Asia, Kabul was under attack from Prince Mirza Sulaiman, the ruler of Badakhshan. With its problems, Kabul was unable to send help to Hindustan, and the Sur Empire easily reconquered Agra and Delhi. Finally, Bairam Khan persuaded the commanders to give him the main command of the Mughal forces, and they all agreed to march against the Sur usurper Sikandar Shah Suri, who ruled in Punjab. However, he proved to be little more than an annoyance to Akbar's army, and he was easily defeated, thus delivering Delhi back into the fold of the Mughal Empire. However, the real threat to Akbar came from Hemu, a Hindu king who used to serve the Sur Empire as a minister. Under his leadership, the Suri army expelled the Mughals from the Indo-Gangetic Plain in 1556, and Delhi was lost once again.

Before Hemu managed to consolidate his power in the region, Bairam Khan reorganized the Mughal army, and with a thirteen-year-old Akbar, he marched to reclaim Delhi. On November 5th, 1556, Hemu was defeated, and the Mughal forces occupied Delhi and Agra soon after that. Hemu was captured and executed, and his head was sent to Kabul to be hanged for everyone to see that young Emperor Akbar had won and regained his empire. Even though Hemu's family and supporters were all executed, Akbar erected a minaret in their remembrance and a memorial for Hemu at the spot where he was beheaded.

Emperor Under Regency (1556–1562)

Depiction of the emperor training an elephant
*https://en.wikipedia.org/wiki/Akbar#/media/File:Kaiser_*
Akbar_b%C3%A4ndigt_einen_Elefanten.jpg

For the first four years of his rule, Akbar didn't take an active role in administering his empire. Instead, he enjoyed hunting far away from his court, and he completely relied on his war commander Bairam Khan, who governed as Wakil-us-Sultanat, an agent of the state. After the defeat of Hemu, Bairam Khan's personal control over the governance only grew, and he gained enough power to place his own Central Asian and Iranian people to key official positions. However, to reward all of his supporters, Bairam Khan needed wealth, and the royal treasuries were quickly emptied. Akbar was seen as a weak ruler because of his young age, and to exploit this Mughal weakness, the Persian Safavids, in 1557, wrestled full control over Kandahar from the Mughals. However, Bairam Khan managed to expand the empire in 1558 when he conquered Ajmer, Jaunpur, and Gwalior.

The emperor enjoyed his hunts, and later in life, he would often combine his military expeditions with hunting. While he was young, he hunted not just for pleasure but also for the practice of martial skills and for gaining influence and reputation among his subordinates. He especially enjoyed *gamarha*, a Mongol-style of hunting in which hundreds or even thousands of horsemen took part. This style of hunting demanded very good organizational and leadership skills in order to perform it with success. Another one of Akbar's pleasures was capturing wild elephants and taming them for battle. In India, elephants were seen as symbols of sovereignty, and it was seen as a special honor to ride this animal into battle. Akbar risked his life very often in his youth just because he wanted to capture, tame, and train his own elephants.

During the period of regency, Akbar devoted time to meet Hindu leaders, and unlike his predecessors, he valued Hindu advice. He didn't rely only on Central Asian and Iranian Muslim commanders. Because of this, many Hindu Rajputs, members of a warrior caste of India, valued Akbar and saw a potential ally in him. They joined the Mughal army, and because they were so well accepted in the Mughal court, they saw it as an opportunity to gather resources and wealth. Later, when Akbar took over the governance of his empire, he would place some of the most loyal Hindu Rajputs into his own household. Among the first Rajputs he met was Bihari Mal, who became the emperor's good friend and whose daughter Akbar would later marry.

Toward Bairam Khan, Akbar was always affectionate, and he treated him with the utmost respect and love as an adoptive father. He even referred to him as Khan Baba, "Noble Father." However, other commanders and courtiers sought to undermine the relationship Akbar had with Bairam Khan. They challenged Bairam's authority and wanted to replace him. Thus, they competed for Akbar's affection throughout his teenage years. There were two main clans that opposed Bairam Khan's authority. One was led by Shamsuddin Muhammad Atgah Khan, better known simply as Ataga Khan, an Afghan soldier who was rewarded with a high position in the Mughal court for saving Humayun's life back in 1540. It was Ataga Khan's wife who was the wet nurse and foster-mother of Akbar, which would make Ataga the emperor's foster-father. Ataga Khan's family remained with Akbar when his parents had to abandon him. They were even with him in the court of Kabul, where Akbar was a royal hostage. It was only natural that Akbar had respect and affection for this family too.

Another faction that opposed Bairam Khan was centered around Akbar's second wet nurse and foster-mother Maham Anga. Together with her relatives, she accused Bairam Khan of arrogance, and she would often cast speculations on Bairam's actions to diminish his prestige. However, Bairam was too proud and often harsh when responding to Maham Anga's accusations, and it led to tensions between him and the young emperor. Throughout his youth, Akbar had no control over the royal treasury, meaning he had no personal wealth to speak of, and it was difficult for him to move against Bairam Khan, who enjoyed all the luxuries of the palace. Once he was challenged, Bairam Khan was ruthless, and he demanded his opposition to beg him for forgiveness. However, Akbar did not approve of such behavior, and he issued a royal decree against Bairam in 1560. Bairam Khan lost many of his supporters, as they saw the decree as a sign of his disgrace and instead joined Akbar. The regent had no other choice than to surrender the symbols of his rank. However, Akbar still loved his Khan Baba, and he gave him a choice: he could stay at his court as an advisor, or he could go to Mecca on a pilgrimage. Bairam chose to go on a pilgrimage, and Akbar assigned him some land properties as his well-deserved pension once he returned from Mecca. However, Bairam Khan never returned to Hindustan again. He also never reached Mecca. He was assassinated in Sindh by a hostile Afghan who retaliated for the death of Hemu.

Even though the clans successfully disposed of Bairam Khan, they continued the struggle over the influence on Akbar's rule. Maham Anga was very successful at dictating politics once she gave her support to Munim Khan, who became the official Vizier (the emperor's advisor and minister of the empire). Munim Khan was an old favorite courtier of Akbar's father, and he helped Maham Anga to promote her son, Adham Khan, in the court. It was during this period, in 1562, to be specific, that the Mughals conquered Malwa from the Rajputs. Also, the Chunar fortress was taken over, which had previously been held by the Indo-Afghans who constantly rebelled. This was when the clash between Adham Khan and Akbar happened, as Anga's son killed the captured women of Chunar instead of sending them to Akbar. He also ordered the assassination of Ataga Khan, his opposer, to gain even more influence and power in the royal court.

The consequence of the clash between Akbar and Adham Khan was that the emperor finally asserted his power, making his courtiers who hungered for power flee the court. Those who constantly schemed and pushed their agendas forward were punished, and Akbar finally started his independent rule, free of regents and power-hungry advisors. Learning his lesson, Akbar did not allow any of his officials to gather too much power. All the authority Bairam Khan once had Akbar divided among his ministers, and now they had to work under the emperor's direct supervision. It is unknown how much power and influence the women of Akbar's court had, but he often listened to the advice of his family members who had no high-ranking status.

It is believed that Akbar suffered dyslexia, as he was illiterate, which was very strange for a person of his rank. But it is recorded that he had an extraordinary memory. He would store all the documents and reports that were read to him in his memory and surprise his officials with the knowledge of the details of outdated documents. He took it upon himself to personally issue every order, promotion, demotion, award, and appointment to his high-ranking officials, commanders, ministers, and courtiers. He also personally took care of many royal marriages, which helped him to create a vast network of new supporters. Akbar also actively took part in planning military strategies and leading his own army. Additionally, Akbar is credited with the invention of many new weapons; however, this could just be an exaggeration from the imperial chroniclers. He made sure to keep up to date with important events by employing news writers who would gather all the important information from all the ministries, the whole empire in general, and even neighboring rulers. And not only did he oversee the people in his kingdom, but he also personally supervised his rich imperial stables, which housed horses, camels, and elephants.

Administration and the Army

Akbar dedicated his rule to the expansion of his empire. As a military empire, the Mughals needed a vast, ever-growing army and an administration that would provide for such an empire. They had to exact tribute and revenues from all the areas they continuously conquered, as the empire demanded a large income to support its army, administration, and Akbar's court. Akbar's predecessors, both Babur and Humayun, seized the treasures of the territories they conquered and also forced the local rulers and landowners to find as many sources of revenue as possible from their territories and give them to the emperor as a tribute. Then the emperor would divide the profits among his loyal commanders to reward them.

Akbar had trouble with many of the local rulers, as they would not comply with his administration. Eventually, he replaced them with those who were more compliant, or their territories would simply be taken and directed by Akbar's administration instead. By doing this, Akbar secured local rulers, Rajputs, and landowners who would give him and his family full support in exchange for protection and the opportunity to rise in political power. Uncultivated lands were granted to prominent people who would turn it into productive lands, who would only start paying tribute to the emperor after they got them up and running. However, the Mughal Empire never established a monopoly over Indian military labor or made a habit of using coercion, and because of it, they often suffered rebellions. During the reign of Akbar, there were 144 rebellions recorded, which were mostly led by local landowners who were free to hire soldiers as they wished.

Although Akbar's predecessors practiced predatory tribute extortion, he was different. Akbar opted for a more centralized model that would exact revenues but be strictly controlled by a set of rules and records, which would supervise both the payers and collectors. He also recruited among the Hindu to fill the new offices of the local administration. Since they were locals, they already possessed the knowledge and experience required for managing the land, and they already had the trust of the local landowners.

Akbar, together with Bairam Khan, modeled his administration on the one used by Sher Shah Suri during his reign of northern India. However, while Bairam Khan spent the gathered revenues to gain supporters, Akbar invested in further modernization and innovation of the administrative and bureaucratic systems. In 1566, Akbar implemented a system of fixed taxes, which were based on the productivity of a territory. But this was extremely hard on the peasants, as the tax rate was fixed according to the imperial court where wealthy people who were able to pay high revenues lived.

Akbar had to decentralize the system and assess a territory's revenue annually, which opened the door for corruption. In 1580, Akbar replaced this system with one called Dahsala, in which revenue was calculated as one-third of the average production of the past ten years. This revenue had to be paid to the emperor in money instead of produce. It was far from a perfect system, but it showed the best results. It needed refining due to the corruption present, and much was done to help fight this corruption and make it possible for both peasants and landowners to prosper. Akbar's administration grouped the areas that produced a similar amount of revenue into a number of assessment groups for easier management, and the local prices were taken into account in order not to agitate the locals who worked the land. If the harvest was destroyed by a flood or drought, the peasants of those affected areas were freed from paying the taxes for that year. The Dahsala system was invented by Raja Todar Mal, a finance minister who worked under both Sher Shah Suri and Akbar. By 1583, the administration and the taxation system were fully implemented throughout the empire.

The landowners of the empire were known as zamindars, and they had the hereditary right to collect and share the produce of their lands, but in turn, they were obliged to provide loans and to improve the agriculture of their regions. They were considered nobles, and they had the right to pass their aristocratic title to their offspring. The zamindars commanded their own army, and since they were often unsatisfied by the Mughal Empire's administration, they would lead rebellions against Emperor Akbar. During the Mughal Empire, all local rulers and Indian princes were called zamindars, whether their titles were actually rai, raja, rana, rao, or rawat. In the Persian world, they were all called zamindars, and the contemporary historian of Akbar's time, Arif Qandhari, figured there were around 300 such rulers under the overlordship of Akbar.

In the army, Akbar implemented a system of ranking for all his high-ranking officers, known as the Mughal mansabdari system. Four centuries earlier, a similar system was used by Akbar's ancestor Genghis Khan, and one had also been used more recently by Sher Shah Suri. Akbar further developed the old system, making it far more sophisticated. This system was implemented in about 1574 when Akbar assigned a numerical grade from 10 to 5,000 to each of his top thousand officers. However, only 33 numerical values were used, each bringing its officer a specific salary.

In turn, the officers had to provide a specific number of cavalry or any other type of soldier, with the number depending on their rank, and they also had to pay for recruited men from their own pockets. Those who ranked with a score of 500 and above were emir, also spelled as amir (noblemen). The system assured every officer that they could move through the ranks during their career and rank higher by performing their duties better.

In the Mughal Empire, the military officers were also given administrative tasks, as the commanders were appointed as governors of newly conquered areas as well. These ranks were not passed down to their successors. An officer could succeed a governor, but he would remain of a lower score until he proved himself more. An office didn't have a specific score, and it would not have been feasible for it to have one, as Akbar often recalled his commanders and appointed new ones. He would suddenly decide to transfer one governor to some other province and assign him to a different administrative office.

The mansab, the grade of an official, wasn't a hereditary system. A father couldn't transfer his mansab to his children, but one's birth did influence the initial ranking of a person. After all, it was by birthright that one would be set on the career path of a commander. Sons always started at a lower rank than their fathers, and they had to prove themselves through hard administrative work and military achievements. But not all new recruits started with the same score. Sons of more prominent officers would start with a higher mansab than those of common soldiers. The princes usually held the highest mansab, scoring higher than anyone else. However, they were not all equal. Their value depended on much more than the score since age, one's family, and the emperor's personal opinion of them made all the difference. The leaders of the newly conquered lands were also given very high initial ranks, as they were kept in their princely positions.

The property of all mansabdars, the soldiers who served under the mansab system, was inherited by the emperor after their death. There would be no inheritance left for the family of the deceased officer, and because of this, mansabdars never built lavish palaces. Instead, they invested their salaries in building temples, mosques, or their own tombs, as these could not be taken by the emperor. However, if Akbar had a favorite among them, he would often give the land and his properties to his family after the officer died. Mansabdars also invested in education, particularly in administrative skills, as well as in his supporters and followers, as these could be passed to his offspring while the land, salary, and household could not.

Akbar's Expansion of the Empire

Akbar started the expansion of his empire when he was only eighteen. He prepared his army to take the southern territories of the Indian subcontinent, namely Rajputana and Malwa, but in 1559, the dispute he had with Bairam Khan put a hold on this military campaign. Once he dismissed Bairam Khan in 1560, Akbar resumed his idea of conquering the south. First came the conquest of Malwa. The conquest was led by Akbar's foster-brother Adham Khan and a commander named Pir Muhammad Khan. Akbar had a claim to this province, as it was part of the Mughal Empire before his father lost it to Sher Shah Suri.

Malwa was ruled by Sultan Baz Bahadur, whose army was defeated by the Mughals in 1561 in the Battle of Sarangpur. In fact, the Afghan forces of Baz Bahadur deserted once they saw the power of the Mughal army when they occupied their capital of Mandu. There, the Mughals massacred the citizens and seized the royal treasury and harem. Akbar even had to intervene and dispose of the bloodthirsty Adham Khan, who, even though he became the governor of the province after the conquest, continued being cruel toward the locals. Baz Bahadur fled to Khandesh, but he was pursued by Pir Muhammad Khan, who was killed after finding himself in the midst of a military clash between two of the Deccan sultanates. This conflict briefly returned Malwa to the rule of Baz Bahadur, but the Mughals returned in 1562 to conquer it once more.

Abdullah Khan Uzbeg was the commander of the renewed conquest of Malwa, but Baz Bahadur managed to escape again. He found refuge in the Gondwana hills, and in 1568, he found shelter at the court of Udai Singh II, the ruler of Mewar. However, Baz Bahadur managed to negotiate his position with the Mughal emperor, and once he surrendered in 1570, he was given a mansab of 2,000 and a position among the Mughal noblemen.

With Malwa now under his control, Akbar was one step closer toward regaining all of the Hindustan territories of his ancestors. However, there was still another northern Indian province that needed to be dealt with in order for Akbar to achieve this victory. Garha was a hilly area in central India; it was sparsely populated and did not have much to offer except a large herd of wild elephants, which was a priceless prize for the Mughal emperor. This province fell in 1564 after its warrior queen, Rana Durgavati, committed suicide when her army was defeated at the Battle of Damoh. With this province, the Mughal Empire was secured, and the whole north of India was once more under the rule of the Mughals.

With all the territories secured, Akbar focused on expanding his kingdom, and the first to suffer an attack was Rajputana. The Mughals already ruled some of the territories of Rajputana, such as Mewat and Ajmer. However, it was time for Abkar to further spread his influence in the heartland of Rajputana, where no other ruler dared to go. He started this conquest in 1561, and most of the territories accepted Akbar's supremacy without much conflict. However, Mewar and Marwar remained unconquered. The leaders of these territories, Udai Singh II and Chandrasen Rathore, respectively, continued to defy Akbar. Udai Singh, as the head of the Sisodia clan, possessed the highest status among the Indian kings, and he was also the descendant of Rana Sanga, who had fought Babur in 1527. Thus, it was imperative for Akbar to make this Indian ruler submit to his authority.

The capital of Mewar was the fortress city of Chittor, and it was a strategically important location because it laid on the shortest route to Gujarat. This means that whoever held Chittor would essentially hold the key to the heartland of Rajputana. When the Mughals attacked, Udai Singh retreated from his court to the hills of Mewar, and he left his capital to be defended by two warriors. In February 1568, the Chittor Fort fell but not before it sustained damage under the four-month-long siege. Akbar beheaded all of the surviving soldiers of Mewar, as well as 30,000 citizens, and displayed their heads on the city towers. This was a common practice during wartime, as the conqueror needed to show off his authority. Udai Singh II's power was completely broken, and he never left his mountain retreat. Akbar didn't bother to pursue him; instead, he left him be.

The next to fall was Rajputana, one of the most powerful fortresses in the subcontinent. In 1568, it fell, but not before its soldiers endured several months of siege. With the taking of Ranthambore, Rajputana was now under Akbar's rule, and most of the kings of these territories submitted to him. Only some clans in Mewar continued to resist, but they were easily dealt with. Once Udai Singh's son Pratap Singh I succeeded his father, he tried to resist Akbar but was defeated at the Battle of Haldighati in 1576. To celebrate the complete submission of Mewar, Akbar rose a new capital city near Agra named it Fatehpur Sikri, "the city of victory." However, Pratap Singh, who survived the battle, continued to rebel against the Mughals. He actually managed to regain most of his father's kingdom while Akbar was still alive.

The next objectives for the Mughal emperor were the territories of Gujarat and Bengal. Both of these territories connected India with Asia, Africa, and Europe, and as such, they were of paramount importance to the trade in India. With the conquest of these territories, Akbar would get rid of the rebelling Mughal nobles who had found refuge in Gujarat, as well as the Afghans under their ruler Sulaiman Khan Karrani in Bengal.

With Rajputana and Malwa now under Akbar's rule, Gujarat was the next to be attacked, as it was surrounded by Mughal territories. Besides having the busiest seaport and being a major trading center in India, Gujarat had fertile and productive lands in its heartland and a well-established textile industry that brought considerable riches to its leaders. Although this was a good reason to conquer this seaside state, Akbar's main motivation was in the fact that in the south of Gujarat was a haven for his Mughal political enemies, who led their rebellions and continued to scheme against him from their bases there. In 1572, Akbar occupied Ahmedabad and other northern cities of Gujarat. When Ahmedabad, the capital of Gujarat, fell, Akbar was proclaimed the official sovereign of the province. His political enemies continued to resist, though, but the emperor managed to drive them out of Gujarat in 1573. All of the coastal cities, including the commercial capital Surat, capitulated to Akbar. Muzaffar Shah III, the king of

Gujarat, hid in a cornfield; after he was found, instead of disposing of him, Akbar gave him a small allowance so he could retire.

After dealing with Gujarat, Akbar was free to turn his focus on Bengal, the last territory under Afghan control. Bengal was ruled by Sulaiman Khan Karrani, who had been a war chieftain under Sher Shah Suri when Humayun was defeated. Sulaiman Khan wanted to avoid any conflict with Akbar and managed to stay independent through diplomatic efforts, but his son, Daud Khan, decided to go on the offensive once he succeeded the Bengal throne in 1572. Sulaiman Khan acknowledged Akbar's supremacy to some extent, which brought peace to his lands. Daud Khan, on the other hand, publicly proclaimed his defiance to Akbar. The Mughal governor of Bihar, a province located next to Bengal, was ordered to deal with Daud Khan, but Akbar felt challenged, and so, he eventually set out to deal with Bengal in person.

Patna, the capital of Bihar, was seized in 1574, and instead of continuing to Bengal, Akbar instructed his generals to carry on the conquest while he returned to Fatehpur Sikri, the new capital. At the Battle of Tukaroi in 1575, the Mughal army won a decisive victory, and Bengal was annexed, as well as the parts of Bihar that were still under the rule of Daud Khan. However, Akbar left the territory of Orrisa as a fief to the Karrani dynasty. Daud Khan rebelled again a year later, though, and he attempted to retrieve the entirety of Bengal, but he didn't have a large base of supporters. However, after his rebellion was defeated, he was forced to flee into exile. Akbar ordered his capture, and soon Daud Khan's head was sent to the emperor.

Military Campaigns in Afghanistan and Central Asia

After the conquest of Bengal and Gujarat, Akbar was occupied with the administrative and military improvement of his empire. It wasn't until 1581 that he organized a big military campaign, though there were always enough rebellions to quell in the meantime, and he found ways to keep his army busy. Mirza Muhammad Hakim, the emperor's brother, invaded Punjab in 1581, but Akbar easily expelled him from the Hindustan territories. However, he didn't think that defeating his brother once was enough, so Akbar continued to pursue Hakim all the way to Kabul, as he wanted to end the threat his brother represented to the Mughal Empire, once and for all.

Akbar had trouble persuading his commanders to leave India and fight a far-off war. Babur once had the problem of persuading his comrades to inhabit India, and now, their descendants didn't want to leave. It was especially hard to persuade the Hindu commanders, as they were forbidden to cross the Indus River due to their traditional beliefs. Hindus of high castes are prohibited, by a religious taboo, from crossing water surfaces as it is believed that by doing so, they will lose their honor and social respect, and thus, they will lose their caste. In the Mughal period, this taboo included rivers, but later it became restricted to only sea voyages. The taboo is known either as kala pani, which literally translates to "black water," or as Samudrolanghana. This taboo still exists in Hinduism, but there are certain rituals one can perform to recover his lost caste after he crosses the water's surface.

To convince his officers, Akbar paid their salaries eight months in advance, which was enough to spur them on. In August, Akbar conquered Kabul, and his brother fled to the mountains. However, Akbar only stayed in Kabul for three weeks. Kabul was then left in the hands of the emperor's sister, Bakht-un-Nisa Begum, while he returned to India. Hakim returned to Kabul after Akbar pardoned him, and he received a high position as an administrative officer. When Muhammad Hakim died in 1585 due to health issues caused by alcoholism, Akbar took Kabul under his direct rule and made it a province of the Mughal Empire.

Akbar moved his capital to Lahore, in the north, in order to be closer to the troublesome areas of his empire. The Uzbeks, now led by Abdullah Khan Shaybanid, continued to be the main threat of the Mughals. Stationed beyond the Khyber Pass, they harassed the borders of the Mughal Empire, but they weren't the only ones. Some Afghan tribes who occupied the border territories often caused unrest in the area, as they were inspired by their new religious leader,

Bayazid Pir Roshan, who founded the Roshaniyya movement to fight against social injustice in the Mughal Empire. Roshan and his followers believed in egalitarianism, or what we would call today communist social systems. To keep Akbar occupied and away from their territories, the Uzbeks paid the Afghans to stir up the situation on their border.

However, there was no major conflict between the Mughals and the Uzbeks, as Akbar managed to negotiate a pact with Abdullah Khan. During this period, the Safavid dynasty held the Khorasan region, in today's Iran, and the Uzbeks wanted to invade the area. In order to do so, they needed the Mughals to not meddle with them. In return, Abdullah Khan promised the Uzbeks would stop supporting the Afghans and would stop offering them refuge from the Mughal Empire. Akbar was ready to deal with the Afghans, and the first attack against them was led by commanders Zain Khan and Raja Birbal. However, their campaign was a disaster, and while retreating over the mountainous area of the Malandarai Pass in 1586, Birbal was killed. Akbar did not wait, and he immediately dispatched another army to contain the Yusufzai, an Afghan tribe, in the mountains. For the next six years, the Mughals were successful in bringing many Afghan war chiefs under their rule.

Akbar still continued to dream about the conquest of Central Asia, especially the territories that make up today's Afghanistan. However, some parts of those territories, such as Badakhshan and Balkh, were under Uzbek rule, and the Mughal emperor wasn't in any haste to break the deal he had made with them. During the 17th century, Akbar's grandson would actually occupy these territories, albeit briefly. Even though his dream of a unified Central Asia wasn't accomplished, Akbar managed to achieve a lot in the territories of the northern frontiers. When Abdullah Khan of the Uzbeks died in 1598, the Mughal rule over the territories of the Afghan tribes was secured, as the threat of the Uzbeks breaking their end of the deal passed. By 1600, the last rebellious Afghan tribe was subdued, and the Roshaniyya movement had been suppressed. All of the prominent people of this movement were exiled, and the son of Roshan, Jalaluddin, was killed in 1601.

During his stay in Lahore in 1586, Akbar dispatched an army to conquer Kashmir in the Upper Indus Basin. Previously, Akbar requested that the ruler of Kashmir, Ali Shah, submit to the Mughal Empire and send his son to be a royal hostage in Akbar's court. When Ali Shah refused, the Mughal emperor saw the opportunity to attack. However, no major conflict happened as Ali Shah surrendered immediately. However, his second son Yaqub raised a rebellion against the Mughals and proclaimed himself king. He resisted submitting to the Mughal emperor for the next three years. Akbar was forced to move from Lahore and deal with this rebellion personally. In June 1589, Yaqub surrendered, and the rebellion ended. The next to fall was the Sindh territory in the Lower Indus Valley. After the Battle of Sehwan in 1591, where the outnumbered Mughals brought defeat to the army of Jani Beg, the ruler of Thatta in southern Sindh, the Mughals had firm control of the whole Indus Valley area.

Akbar also led military campaigns against the Safavid dynasty in Kandahar and the Deccan sultans. The Deccan sultanates were five kingdoms occupying the territories of the Deccan Plateau: Ahmednagar, Berar, Bidar, Bijapur, and Golconda. They all eventually submitted to Akbar after they were defeated by the superior Mughal army. Kandahar was conquered in 1595, and the Deccan sultans were defeated by 1601. Akbar was so successful in his expansion of the Mughal Empire that by 1605, he ruled a large swath of territory, extending from the Bay of Bengal to Kandahar and Badakhshan. His territories bordered the western sea in Sindh, and from there, his influence spread well into central India.

Chapter 5 – One Hundred Years of the Mughal Empire (1605–1707)

Akbar died on October 27th, 1605. He had been suffering from dysentery since October 3rd and was unable to recover. After his death, Akbar was buried in Sikandra, Agra, in a tomb that was an architectural marvel at the time.

The Mughal Empire he left was a secular empire that wanted to emphasize cultural integration. In India, Akbar is praised as a powerful leader who did not rely only on his military power but also on diplomacy. However, in Pakistan, he is often forgotten and not even mentioned as it is believed he weakened Islam with his religious tolerance. Akbar not only accepted Hinduism as the rightful religion of his empire, but he also invited two Christian Jesuits to preach Christianity. However, once they started condemning Islam and speaking against the prophet Muhammad, they were forced to leave the empire.

Akbar was succeeded by his son, Nur-ud-din Muhammad Salim. He wasn't the eldest son, but he was the only surviving one, as the others had died during their infancy. Salim Mirza was known to enjoy earthly pleasures, such as alcohol and his harem. He had twenty wives while he was still a prince and numerous concubines. He was persuaded by his advisors to rebel against Emperor Akbar, and he led an army to start a civil war right before Akbar's death. However, when Akbar fell ill, Salim Mirza made peace with his father. Salim was also known for his cruelty as he liked to torture his enemies. He was a disobedient son, and Akbar tried to reform him and prepare him for the succession. However, Akbar started favoring his grandson, Khusrau Mirza, instead. He even voiced the idea of making Khusrau his successor and renouncing Salim. However, Akbar had no time to make his will as he suddenly fell ill and soon died.

Jahangir (r. 1605–1627)

Portrayal of Jahangir
https://en.wikipedia.org/wiki/Jahangir#/media/File:Indian_-
_Single_Leaf_of_a_Portrait_of_the_Emperor_Jahangir
_-_Walters_W705_-_Detail.jpg

In September 1605, Salim Mirza was crowned the Mughal emperor, and he took the name Jahangir, the "World-Conqueror." Khusrau Mirza challenged his father's succession, stating that he was Akbar's choice, but his father imprisoned him in the fort of Agra. As a punishment, Jahangir blinded his son by piercing his eyes with wires.

Some sources say the Mughal emperor continued to be cruel toward his first son, saying that he would bring Khusrau in chains wherever he traveled. Jahangir expected his son to appear before him each day and offer his respect, but Khusrau continued to defy him. Finally, he gave the prince to his younger son, Khurram Mirza, who killed Khusrau in order to clear his own path to succession.

As an emperor, Jahangir was determined to rise above his predecessors. He improved his father's imperial model, but he also strived to centralize the government around himself, as he thought of an emperor as a holy figure, closer to the divine than his subjects. When Jahangir rose to the throne of the Mughal Empire, he inherited the treasures that came with it, and he used these riches to gain new supporters by raising their salaries and rewarding the officials who pleased him.

To show off his power, Jahangir issued new coins, increasing their size by 20 percent. However, this decision proved to be destructive for the economy of the Mughal Empire, and after only six years, Jahangir returned to the old standard size of the coins. Although his ideas were not always successful, Jahangir continued to innovate coinage. He was proud of his idea to decorate the coins with a zodiac sign for the month of its production. Some coins had his own portrait, complete with a wine glass, and it was these coins that offended many orthodox Muslims, who were against alcohol consumption. Although Jahangir was a renowned consumer of both alcohol and drugs, which led him to suffer serious health issues, he would often ban the production of both under the excuse of religious piety.

Just as his predecessor Babur had, Jahangir kept a personal journal in which he detailed his daily life. Because he never had his journal revised, we are left with the evidence of all of the emperor's thoughts, mood swings, and attitudes. He described his opium and alcohol addiction, as well as the health consequences they left on him. By the age of 26, Jahangir's hands shook so badly that he had to be fed by his attendees. Even a cup of tea had to be brought to his mouth. He got to the point where he had to consume the drug in order to be able to function.

In his journal, Jahangir also described the business of the Mughal Empire, especially trade. The Portuguese were already established on the west coast of the Indian subcontinent, and together with the British East India Company, and later with the Dutch East India Company, they increased the economy of the Mughal Empire with foreign trade. There was a high demand for Indian textiles and other products in Europe, and they were spending their silver from the Americas on buying and investing in Indian production. In return, crops from America entered India, such as maize and tobacco, which were then grown in the fields of the Mughal Empire. Although Emperor Akbar didn't believe in the health benefits of tobacco, it was actually Jahangir who banned its consumption at his court, claiming that it brought a disturbance in people's temperaments and constitutions.

Though he launched a few military campaigns, Jahangir never engaged in the wars personally. Instead, he enjoyed traveling the empire and admiring the beauty of its nature and art. Although some contemporary scholars accused him of cowardice, it wasn't necessarily essential for the emperor to be present on the battlefield in order for the campaign to be successful. In fact, modern historians think his absence from the battlefield is a display of the stability in the Mughal Empire. Jahangir continued to expand the empire throughout his reign, and his armies were all victorious on the northern, western, and eastern borders. However, he failed to completely integrate the newly conquered territories, which would later lead to the weakening of the empire.

In 1594, while he was still just a prince, Akbar sent Jahangir to deal with the Sisodia Rajputs of Mewar, who continued to defy the Mughal Empire. But Jahangir had little success then, and once he became the emperor, he sent his second son, Parviz, to end the campaign. Parviz also failed, and it was Jahangir's third son, Khurram, who finally negotiated the submission of the ruler of Mewar, Rana Amar Singh I, on February 5th, 1615. Rana Amar Singh was the most powerful of the Rajput leaders at the time, and it was essential for the Mughal Empire to show its dominance over Mewar. The Rajput leader was hard to break, though, and the whole Mughal court had to be moved to Ajmer from 1613 to 1616 in order to support the campaign against Mewar. In 1616, the Mughals won against the rebels of the Deccan frontier. Even though Parviz Mirza had previously conquered the city of Ahmednagar in 1605, the area continued to be affected by the stubborn rebellions against the Mughal Empire.

Jahangir died in 1627 after he had suffered a severe cold during his journey from Kabul to Kashmir. As he was so far away from Lahore, where he had commissioned his tomb to be built, his entrails were taken out in order to preserve the body, and they were buried at Baghsar Fort in Kashmir. His body was then sent to be buried in Shahdara Bagh, a suburb of Lahore. Jahangir is widely perceived as a weak and incapable ruler. Scholars see him as a man that was not fit to be an emperor, and they all agree he would have been a happier man if he was left to deal with the arts and nature, as those remained his passions throughout his life. Jahangir had a habit of retreating to his private life in order to avoid his duties as an emperor. Although he wished to be better than all of his predecessors, he couldn't keep up with a life that wasn't suitable for him. To compensate for his dissatisfaction, he indulged in opium and wine, which only brought even more laziness and apathy for his empire.

Shah Jahan (r. 1628–1658)

Shah Jahan, the fifth Mughal emperor
*https://en.wikipedia.org/wiki/Shah_Jahan#/media/File:'Jujhar_Singh_*
*Bundela_Kneels_in_Submission_to_Shah_Jahan',_painted_by_*
Bichitr,_c._1630,_Chester_Beatty_Library_(cropped).jpg

Even before the death of Emperor Jahangir, his third son, Shahab-ud-din Muhammad Khurram (mentioned above as Khurram Mirza), rebelled. Jahangir married a widowed daughter of a Persian noble, Nur Jahan, in 1611. She became an extremely influential person in the court, and thus, the young prince resented her. She married her daughter from her first marriage to Shahzada Shahryar, Khurram's youngest brother, and then used her influence to promote him as the next emperor. Enraged, Khurram Mirza raised an army in 1622 and started a rebellion against his father, who had fallen under the spell of his scheming wife, Nur Jahan.

However, in March of 1623, the young prince was defeated, and he had to seek refuge in Mewar, where Maharaja Karan Singh II took him in. Even though his rebellion wasn't successful, and he ultimately had to submit to his father, Khurram continued to resent his stepmother, and the tension between the two continued to grow. Since the inheritance of the Mughal Empire was not regulated by the law of primogeniture, the princes had to earn the inheritance of the throne through their military successes and through the power and influence they had in the court. This means that rebellions and civil wars were common in the empire.

Even though Nur Jahan used her influence to install her own brother, Asaf Khan, as the vizier, once Jahangir died, her plans of succession were unfruitful. Asaf Khan was a supporter of Khurram, and he ensured his sister's confinement once the emperor was dead. Asaf Khan also expertly managed all the court intrigues to assure the accession of Khurram Mirza, who took the regnal name Shah Jahan, "King of the World." The first action of the new emperor was to put to death everyone who opposed him and to place his stepmother under arrest. To secure his position as emperor, Shah Jahan executed his half-brother Shahryar, his nephews Dawar and Garshasp, and the sons of his older brother, Khusrau Mirza, who had been executed much earlier. Even though the sons of the late prince Daniyal Mirza, who died due to complications of alcoholism, did not oppose him directly, Shah Jahan decided to kill them nonetheless so he could rule the empire free of any threats.

Shah Jahan inherited his father's almost empty royal treasury, but he was determined to show off his power and the stability of his empire through lavish ceremonies, artwork, and architecture. He constructed a magnificent throne, known as the Peacock Throne, which was lavishly decorated with various gems and gold. It took him seven years to gather all the needed precious stones for the throne. Shah Jahan also invested heavily in architecture. Even though many magnificent structures of Mughal architecture were built on his orders, the most magnificent is still considered to be the Taj Mahal, located in the city of Agra. It was commissioned in 1632, and it was intended to be a tomb for his favorite wife, Mumtaz Mahal. The stories of their love still fill the pages of Indian literature. The Taj Mahal also serves as his own tomb, as he requested to be buried next to his favorite wife.

To finance all of his architectural projects, Shah Jahan lowered the base salary of his mansabdars, even if they were of higher ranks. This decision would lead to political instability later in his rule. However, the military of the Mughal Empire remained strong. The various sources from 1648 state that the army of Shah Jahan consisted of 911,400 infantry, musketeers, and artillery soldiers and of 185,000 sowars, a Mughal title for cavalry units. It was Shah Jahan who introduced the Marwari horses into the army, as they were his favorite breed. He also commissioned the mass production of cannons, making his empire a military machine. To be able to supply such a huge army, he had to increase the taxes he demanded from his citizens. And even though his economic decisions had a huge impact on the later years of his rule, the Mughal Empire was generally very stable.

Shah Jahan continued the steady expansion of the empire that his father had previously initiated. His own sons led military campaigns, especially to the north and west. The emperor also annexed the kingdoms of Baglana, Mewar, and Bundelkhand. In the territories of the Deccan sultanates, Shah Jahan captured Daulatabad Fort in 1632. Other Deccan sultanates soon followed: Golconda submitted to Shah Jahan in 1635, and Bijapur did so the next year. Shah Jahan appointed his son, Aurangzeb, as the viceroy of the Deccan, and Aurangzeb would later go on to conquer the rebelling Baglana, Golconda, and Bijapur in 1656 and 1657.

Shah Jahan knew, from his own experience, that once the time came, the succession wars between his sons would start. He wanted to prolong the period of peace for as long as he could and postpone the succession drama until after his death. He had four sons, and even though he favored his eldest, Dara Shikoh, he wanted to protect his other sons. Dara was kept close to the court, as his father felt the need to personally prepare him for the rule. He awarded his eldest with various dignities and titles, which demonstrated to others that he was the heir apparent. Both Dara and the emperor's favorite daughter, Jahanara, were children of his first and favorite wife, Mumtaz Mahal. The siblings were very close, and Jahanara openly supported her brother in the succession wars.

The rest of the sons of Shah Jahan were dispatched throughout the empire to serve as viceroys and commanders. Even though they were far away from the throne, they gathered much-needed experience and support for the later clash with their brother. Shah Shuja, the second eldest, was appointed as the governor of Bengal and Orissa in 1638. Bengal was one of the richest and most powerful regions of the empire, and Shah Shuja built his base there. Shah Jahan's fourth son, Murad Bakhsh, proved to be inadequate as he often misjudged the situations in the regions appointed to him for governance, which were Multan, Kashmir, Deccan, Kabul, Malwa, and Gujarat.

Shah Jahan's third son, Aurangzeb, was the most successful of the three brothers who governed the empire. He commanded the forces of Deccan successfully, conquering the whole plateau. Even though Aurangzeb's military successes were important, he received much less recognition than all of his brothers. However, he gained the loyalty of the Mughal's most powerful and battle-hardened army, which fought the constant rebellions of the Deccan sultanates.

When Shah Jahan fell ill in September 1657, Dara proclaimed himself as his father's regent. Even though the emperor recovered fairly quickly, the three younger brothers had already conspired against Dara and made a pact. Together, they decided to attack Dara, and in 1658, the first battle occurred. Shah Shuja attacked Dara first, not waiting to be united with the forces of his brothers. Dara easily defeated him, and while Shuja fled back to Bengal, the forces of Murad Bakhsh and Aurangzeb attacked the imperial army of their eldest brother. This time, Dara lost, and Murad proclaimed himself emperor. However, it was Aurangzeb who pressed forward and imprisoned Shah Jahan in Agra. The emperor proposed peace and promised that he would divide the empire between his four sons. However, Aurangzeb was too powerful, and he captured and executed

Murad in 1661. And since he had already crushed Shuja in 1659, who was later assassinated while fleeing his brother's forces, he only had Dara left to deal with.

Defeated, Dara could only run, and he sought refuge in Punjab, Sindh, Gujarat, and Rajasthan, where he was finally defeated by Aurangzeb. Dara was captured and executed in 1662. After defeating all of his brothers, Aurangzeb kept his father Shah Jahan imprisoned in the fort of Agra. The old emperor had no real support of the army or the nobles of his court. Instead, he was attended by his favorite daughter Jahanara, who remained unmarried. Shah Jahan died in 1666 at the age of 74 from natural causes. Aurangzeb was already in full control of the Mughal Empire by this point, and there was no one left to challenge his right to the throne.

Aurangzeb (r. 1658–1707)

Aurangzeb
https://upload.wikimedia.org/wikipedia/commons/b/b3/Aurangzeb-portrait.jpg

Muhi-ud-Din Muhammad is more commonly known by his nickname Aurangzeb, "Ornament of the Throne," even though his regnal title was Alamgir, "Conqueror of the World." He ruled for 49 years, during which he expanded his empire and ruled almost the whole Indian subcontinent. He is considered to be the last effective ruler of the Mughal empire and the one who established Sharia law throughout India. Though he is praised for his military genius, he is also described as the most controversial ruler in Indian history.

Aurangzeb was 26 years old when he resigned from the governorship of the Deccan Plateau to pursue a life of religious devotion. However, after only six months, his father ordered him to resume his duties. Aurangzeb was extremely religious, and once he took the throne, he began cleansing the court of the unorthodox protocols of his predecessors. His goal was to make Islam the dominant religion in his empire, and he was relentless in his endeavors. Today, many scholars accuse him of the attempt to destroy the Bamiyan Buddhas when he tried to use cannons to bring down the statues. He managed to break the legs of the Buddhas before his attention was brought elsewhere. He severely punished the temples and schools of the Hindu Brahmins, a caste of Hindu priests, ordering their demolition throughout the provinces. Aurangzeb also punished the Muslims who didn't respect the Islamic laws on proper dressing, and he executed many Sufi mystics who opposed his endeavors to bring Islam to the forefront of the empire. Sikh Guru Tegh Bahadur was publicly killed in 1675 for resisting the forced mass conversion of Hindus to Islam.

Even though Aurangzeb introduced Sharia Law in the Mughal Empire, and despite his efforts to convert the non-Muslims, he employed more Hindu bureaucrats than any of his predecessors. Scholars believe that it was his successful campaign in Deccan back in 1656 and 1657 that caused the constant influx of Marathas (from present-day Maharashtra) to the Mughal Empire. One of the Rajput nobles was even known for the destruction of mosques in order to build Hindu temples, and in spite of knowing about this, Aurangzeb continued to work with him for the next two decades. Only the death of this Rajput ended their good relationship.

Since Aurangzeb's father led a very lavish life, causing Aurangzeb to inherit an almost empty royal treasury, Aurangzeb imposed a jizya in 1679. This was a military tax on non-Muslim citizens who did not fight for the Mughal Empire. However, women, children, the elderly, the handicapped, the ill, the mentally ill, monks, hermits, and slaves were all exempt from this new tax. Also, the non-Muslims who were only temporary residents (mainly the merchants) of the empire did not need to pay the tax. However, Hindu merchants had to pay their taxes at a higher rate than Muslims. In addition, all Hindus were removed from their offices in the revenue administration. There are contemporary historians who claim that the jizya was just a tax on paper that was forced on the people of the Mughal Empire.

Aurangzeb mainly ruled from the city of Shahjahanabad (Old Delhi) until 1679, when he left. He did not see this city ever again, nor did he ever come back to the territories of Hindustan. Until the end of his rule, Aurangzeb would move among military encampments or reside in the provisional capitals of certain regions to deal with emerging crises personally. Sometimes, he would even command the battles himself.

The Mughal emperor tried to meddle in the succession disputes of Rajasthan when he took the only surviving son of the dead Maharaja Jaswant Singh Rathore of Marwar. He converted the infant to Islam and named him Muhammadi Raj. He also selected a new leader for Marwar, an unpopular nephew of Jaswant Singh. The population objected to Aurangzeb's interference, and the clan of Rathore rebelled. Marwar was annexed because of this rebellion, which Aurangzeb personally oversaw. Neighboring Mewar had to quickly react unless they wanted the same destiny as Marwar, and the Sisodia clan of Mewar decided to join the rebellion.

Aurangzeb appointed his fourth son, Muhammad Akbar, as the commander of the Mughal armies that fought the rebels. However, in 1681, Akbar switched sides and joined the Marwars, proclaiming himself the new emperor. Akbar almost imprisoned his father, but his own Rathore allies were persuaded to betray him. Aurangzeb defeated his son, but instead of begging for forgiveness, Akbar sought refuge in the south at the court of the Maratha leader, Maharaja Sambhaji.

Furious, Aurangzeb imprisoned his favorite daughter Zeb-un-Nissa, accusing her of conspiring with Akbar. After spending twenty years in prison, Zeb-un-Nissa died, but the year of her death is debated to be either 1701 or 1702. Once the Sisodia rana of Mewar died, his successor gave up on fighting Aurangzeb and ceded his territories. However, Marwar continued to fight the Mughal Empire, using guerilla warfare strategies, and the fighting continued until Aurangzeb's death in 1707.

Akbar continued to defy his father, even after they reconciled when Aurangzeb offered him forgiveness for the rebellion. Akbar launched failed raids into Hindustan and taunted his father, often reminding Aurangzeb of the fact that his own son had overthrown him. He also urged him to renounce the throne and go make the Hajj, an Islamic pilgrimage to Mecca. Akbar had to run away from his father's anger once more, and he fled to the court of the Safavid dynasty, just like his ancestors Babur and Humayun had done. However, unlike his ancestors, Akbar did not return to Hindustan as a conqueror. Instead, he died in exile in 1706, and he didn't live long enough to succeed his father.

Aurangzeb sent his second son, Muhammad Mu'azzam, to capture Hyderabad in the wealthy Golconda Sultanate, which he did in 1685. However, the sultan retreated to the impregnable Golconda Fort, and Mu'azzam wasn't able to defeat him. Convinced that his son had betrayed him, Aurangzeb took direct command of the forces, and it took him eight months to bring down the fortress. Mu'azzam, his wife, and his children were imprisoned for betrayal in 1687, and they were not released until 1695. When Golconda fell, the sultanate was annexed, and Aurangzeb took its rich treasury. The Muslims of the Golconda court were received into the Mughal military service, and they were given a mansab of 1,000 or higher, depending on their previous level of prestige.

During his seventies and eighties, Aurangzeb struggled to control his empire. The Mughals had expanded their territories to the point where the costs of the empire exceeded the benefits for its subjects.

The emperor simply had no adequate administration, technology, or manpower to rule such a vast empire. Instead of continuing to expand the Mughal Empire, Aurangzeb was forced to satisfy his army by raiding the surrounding kingdoms. They would occasionally make those kingdoms pay a yearly tribute, but Aurangzeb was aware he could not afford to annex them and have their territories join with the already swollen Mughal Empire.

Aurangzeb knew he could not rule forever, but he was displeased with all of his sons and didn't consider any of them worthy of his throne. He continued to keep them bound to him through monetary allowances, often sending them to govern the lands that would bring the least revenue. By the time Aurangzeb had aged, and the time for deciding the succession was evident, none of his sons was strong enough to take the empire under his own rule. Because Aurangzeb had ruled for so long—he was 88 when he died—his sons were already old, with Mu'azzam being 63 and Azam, Aurangzeb's third youngest son, 54. So, the two princes were forced to wait until their father's death to be able to make their moves and fight for the throne.

Aurangzeb saw no other way to preserve his empire but to divide it between his sons. In his will, he dedicated the provinces of Agra, Ajmer, Aurangabad, Berar, Bidar, Gujarat, Khandesh, and Malwa to one son, while the other would get Delhi along with the provinces of Allahabad, Oudh (Awadh), Bengal, Bihar, Kabul, Kashmir, Multan, Orissa, Punjab, and Thatta. His only other surviving son, who was also the youngest, was the son of a low-born concubine. He already had Golconda and Bijapur under his command, and Aurangzeb asked Azam and Mu'azzam to respect their youngest brother, Muhammad Kam Bakhsh. However, the events that followed couldn't be controlled by Aurangzeb's sons or by any of the later emperors of the Mughal Empire. Many consider the year 1707, the year when Aurangzeb died, to be the last year of the Mughal Empire because, after this date, a series of weak emperors ruled. However, the dynasty continued, and the contemporary warlords and regional rulers recognized its importance, albeit nominally.

Chapter 6 – The Decline and Fragmentation of the Empire (1707–1857)

Stating in his will that the empire needed to be divided, Aurangzeb tried to spare his sons from the succession wars that he had to win when it was his time to rule. However, all three princes, Mu'azzam, Azam, and Kam Bakhsh, declared themselves the emperor of the whole Mughal Empire. Even though the brothers wanted to kill each other in the power struggle, none of them had control over a large military force. This was due to Aurangzeb lowering the salary of the mansabdars, causing commanders to protect their own interests. This doesn't mean they didn't recognize the legitimacy of the princes, and they avoided direct disobedience, but whenever it was possible, they avoided fighting other powerful commanders.

It was Mu'azzam that reached Shahjahanabad and Agra first, and by taking the royal treasuries there, he proclaimed himself Emperor Bahadur Shah I (r. 1707–1712). Soon, he clashed with Azam, who marched with his army from the Deccan Plateau to Shahjahanabad, but Azam was killed during the battle. The third son, Kam Bakhsh, fortified himself in Golconda, but in 1709, Bahadur Shah launched an attack and killed him, thus securing his throne.

After every succession struggle, the new ruler would need money, and Bahadur Shah was no exception. To get more wealth, he extracted more revenues than his predecessors. The territories that were controlled by his brothers were divided among his most loyal mansabdars as a reward. The Rajputs of Rajasthan and the Sikhs in Punjab took the opportunity of the power struggle to raise their own rebellions, and Bahadur Shah spent most of his ruling years in campaigns to quell them. However, the emperor lacked the bond his predecessors had with their mansabdars and subjects, and his four-year rule was just the beginning of the empire's downfall.

Bahadur Shah died of illness, probably due to the enlargement of his spleen, on February 27th, 1712, and a new succession war started. All of his four sons proclaimed themselves as the new emperor, just like Bahadur Shah and his brothers had done. In their desperation to gain the loyalty of the mansabdars, they spent enormous amounts of money on bribing the right people and spending it on their personal armies. In the beginning, the three brothers conspired to divide the empire between themselves once they killed the fourth, Azim-ush-Shan, who was more powerful than the others as he had accumulated much wealth as the governor of Bengal. However, once they killed Azim-ush-Shan, the three brothers turned against each other. Finally, after the bloodthirsty conflicts and fratricide had played out, the eldest, Muhammad Mu'izz-ud-Din, better known as his regnal title of Jahandar Shah, emerged victorious in 1713. However, within months, the son of the late Azim-ush-Shan, Muhammad Farrukhsiyar, marched his forces down the Ganges from Bengal and attacked his uncle. Near Agra, he defeated the imperial army and seized the throne for himself. During his rule, which lasted from 1713 to 1719, he struggled to hold the vast empire together.

The Salatin (1713–1859)

In 1713, Jahandar Shah created the Salatin, the slums of the Red Fort. The term was also used for all the Mughal princes who lived, along with their families, in the Red Fort, located in the city of Delhi. Emperor Jahandar Shah made them all prisoners of the Red Fort by confining them to slum-like quarters, and he passed a law that wouldn't allow the princes and the members of their families to leave the fort. Although they lived the shameful lives of prisoners, the people of the Mughal Empire still believed they held a privileged status.

Since each emperor had a large harem, the number of imprisoned relatives grew over time. The recorded number of Salatin in 1836 was 795, but by 1848, the number had increased to 2,104. All of them lived in the Red Fort and were guarded by eunuchs, who would lock them in their quarters during the night. Attempts to escape were made, but they were treated as criminals regardless. Some princes managed to escape, and they had to seek refuge in the neighboring kingdoms, where they were often treated as royal guests. However, those who remained in Salatin lived in perpetual poverty. Emperors did allow them small allowances, though, which would keep them dependent on their goodwill. However, that was not nearly enough money to keep the whole family alive. Instead, Salatins would often turn to moneylenders for help.

Oftentimes, the emperors would exhaust their riches, and they couldn't even pay the small allowance of one to five rupees per day to his imprisoned relatives. The amount of the allowance depended on how close a relative was to the ruling emperor. Salatins would protest with loud crying and wailing inside their home, which would drive the ruling emperor mad enough to borrow from moneylenders just to be able to pay his relatives. A British Army engineer, named Major Alexander Cunningham, visited the Red Fort, and he described how the Salatins lived. He recorded that a high wall was erected around the slums to keep the world of the Salatins very private. They lived in mat huts with only a few objects in their private possessions. They were all starved and half-naked. Among them were older people, some even in their eighties, and infants. Sometimes, they were given a few blankets to keep them warm during the cold months, and these were seen as an act of charity by the emperor.

At one point, the East India Company tried to resolve the issue of the Salatin but ultimately failed. They proposed to open a school within the walls of the Red Fort, in which they would educate the Mughal princes and give them the opportunity to find a job working for the Company. However, they couldn't guarantee a job for everyone, as there were so many of them. Those who wouldn't receive employment would just create additional problems for the Company, and so, the plan was abandoned. The Salatins were to stay imprisoned and all but forgotten.

When the last emperor of the Mughal Empire died in 1862, the Salatins were finally free to leave the Red Fort. Entire families wandered from one place to another, not being able to settle in the vast world that was completely unknown to them. It took time for them to finally disappear in the crowd, forgetting who they were. Occasionally, a family would claim they were the descendants of the Salatins, but no one was interested in them anymore. The world had changed, and the Mughal royal family meant nothing to the people.

During its decline, the emperor kept the nominal authority of the Mughal Empire; however, the effective military and political power were in the hands of prominent courtiers, commanders, and governors. Farrukhsiyar took the throne with the help of the governors of Allahabad and Bihar. They were actually brothers, Sayyid Abdullah Khan and Sayyid Husain Ali Khan Barha, and they were both excellent military tacticians. However, Farrukhsiyar had no riches to reward the brothers who supported his enthronement, and as he had no private army, he couldn't confront the Sayyid brothers. They posed a serious problem, as they threatened to enthrone another royal family member whenever Farrukhsiyar proved to be too demanding of their revenues. Farrukhsiyar schemed to lower the influence of the Sayyid brothers by favoring other mansabdars, most often Nizam-ul-Mulk, the leader of the Turani family that governed the territories in the Deccan Plateau.

Although Farrukhsiyar sought the support of the Rajputs and other Hindu commanders, some of them rebelled against him. Raja Ajit Singh Rathore expelled the Mughal officials from Marwar and Ajmer. He was aided by the Rajputs of Mewar and Amber, who also rebelled. Again, the emperor needed the help of the Sayyid brothers to quell the rebellions in the Deccan, and after succeeding, he married the daughter of Ajit Singh in 1715. However, he followed the example of his orthodox Muslim predecessor Aurangzeb, and he converted his new wife to Islam. Once she was widowed, she went through the purification ceremony and returned to Hinduism, becoming an avid opposer of the Mughal culture.

The Sayyid brothers continued to support Farrukhsiyar, but in reality, they were the true rulers. The emperor was just a figurehead, although he continuously tried to regain political power. As he had no power to manage the events that followed, he decided to spend most of his time hunting, writing poetry, and scheming to free himself from the too-powerful Sayyids, as well as from the influence of their powerful enemies. It is reported that the emperor tried to poison some of the most powerful mansabdars and that he would also appoint two men to the same office in the hopes that they would kill each other.

Finally, the Sayyid brothers had had enough of the emperor's efforts to dispose of them, and in 1719, they decided to overthrow him and place a more compliant emperor on the throne. They already had the reputation of being kingmakers due to their previous efforts to help Farrukhsiyar. On February 28th, they dragged the emperor out of his harem and blinded him. At first, they believed it was enough to just imprison Farrukhsiyar, but they changed their minds, and the emperor was assassinated on April 19th. In his place, the Sayyid brothers appointed Rafi ud-Darajat, the tenth Mughal emperor.

The Sayyid brothers destroyed the concept of an individual rule in the Mughal Empire, and their actions would be imitated by other powerful families of the Mughal court. In total, the Mughal court would see seven depositions in the next forty years. The Sayyids grasped too much power and created enemies who would unite against them. Even though both were assassinated in the times that followed, they created the pattern of kingmaking that would continue to happen under the supervision of various powerful commanders of the Mughal Empire. Some scholars even named them regents of the empire, though such a title was never officially given to them. All of the Mughal emperors who ruled after Farrukhsiyar were no more than puppets of their courtiers, and they were all chosen from the slums of the Salatin.

In the decades that followed the assassination of Farrukhsiyar, the Salatin emperors were constantly afraid for their lives. Kingmakers were ruthless in using these poor Mughal princes, enthroning them and disposing them at their will. Some of them were assassinated, while others were returned to the slums from which they came, grateful that their lives were spared. The majority of them ruled for only a few months, but there was one that ruled for almost thirty years, Muhammad Shah, though he was also one of the weakest Mughal emperors. None of the Salatin princes had any administrative knowledge or military experience to rule the empire, which made them perfect rulers for the powerful families of the empire who would ultimately control them.

Muhammad Shah (r. 1719–1748)

Muhammad Shah
https://en.wikipedia.org/wiki/Muhammad_Shah#/media/
File:Mu%E1%B8%A5ammad_Sh%C3%A1h_on_horseback.jpg

Born Nasir-ud-Din Muhammad Shah, he was imprisoned together with his mother by his uncle, Jahandar Shah. He was only twelve when the succession war between his uncles and father took place, and even though he was confined in the slums of Salatin, his mother took care of his education and gave him the best she could. Perhaps this was the reason why the Sayyid brothers chose him as the emperor in 1719. After they disposed of Farrukhsiyar, several Salatin princes were chosen, but they only reigned for a few months before Muhammad Shah ascended the throne.

Muhammad Shah was enthroned in the Red Fort on September 29th, 1719, and like his predecessors, the Sayyid brothers kept him under strict supervision. Although he was free to finally leave Salatin and live the rich life of the emperor, Muhammad Shah wasn't free to make a single decision on his own. The first challenge to his throne happened the very next year, in 1720, when the political enemy of the Sayyid brothers, Nizam-ul-Mulk, later known as Asaf Jah I once he established the Hyderabad state and his own dynasty, chose Muhammad Ibrahim as the new Mughal emperor. However, both Asaf Jah and Ibrahim were quickly defeated by the ever-growing supporters of Muhammad Shah.

Although he was very young, Muhammad Shah was aware of the politics of the Sayyid brothers, and he strived to get rid of their influence. After the defeat of Muhammad Ibrahim, the Mughal emperor made a deal with Asaf Jah I, and Sayyid Husain Ali Khan was assassinated in October of 1720 as a consequence of that deal. Muhammad Shah now took full control over the Mughal army, and he sent Asaf Jah to take command of the Mughal provinces in the Deccan. Another noble, Muhammad Amin Khan Turani, was given a mansab of 8,000, and he was sent to confront Grand Vizier Sayyid Abdullah Khan. In the Battle of Hasanpur on November 15th, 1720, the second Sayyid brother was defeated and captured. The Mughal emperor would decide to execute him two years later.

Muhammad Shah was now finally free of the Sayyid brothers' influence; however, he lacked the knowledge of how to run his empire. Asaf Jah was appointed as the grand vizier, but when Muhammad Shah displayed an ultimate disinterest and inability to deal with the administration of the empire, Asaf Jah left the court in disgust. Instead of taking the opportunity to rule the Mughal Empire either from the shadows or by directly disposing of Muhammad Shah, Asaf Jah decided to take the territories of Deccan and founded his state of Hyderabad in 1724.

Even though Muhammad Shah had gained control of his empire by getting rid of the control imposed by the Sayyid brothers, he was still considered to be a weak ruler. During his reign, much of the destabilization of the Mughal Empire happened. For the most part, the emperor himself contributed to the problem due to his lack of knowledge and wisdom to run the state. The fragmentation of the empire, which began with the creation of Hyderabad State, would not stop. Although the decline of the empire could already be felt, it continued to be strong in at least one aspect: culture. Muhammad Shah was a great patron of the arts, and he was even famous for his writing, which he did under the pen name Sada Rangila, "Ever Joyous."

It was during his rule that Urdu replaced the Persian script, as Muhammad Shah proclaimed it to be the language of his court. He was a great patron of music, especially Sufi Islamic Qawwali, which was Sufi devotional music that gained popularity and spread throughout the empire and the rest of Southeast Asia. Muhammad Shah also opened schools, as he valued education, but he also translated the Quran in simple Persian and Urdu, thus making it available to the masses. The Quran was then taught in the elementary schools that Muhammad Shah opened, known as *maktabs*. Muhammad Shah spent riches employing famous artists, from painters to musicians. The arts were taught at the court, and it paved the road for the development of Indian classical music. In fact, the Mughal emperor spent more money investing in art than in the administration of the state, which only helped to ensure the later fragmentation of the government.

The Later Mughal-Maratha Wars, which lasted between 1728 and 1763, consisted of raids from Malwa that continuously devastated the north of the ill-administered Mughal Empire. These conflicts taught Muhammad Shah the importance of the empire's administration. He managed to get rid of the bad advisors who had multiplied around him after Asaf Jah left, and he was forced to adopt the skills of statesmanship. However, the fragmentation of his vast empire had already started, and he could do next to nothing to stop it. In the Punjab region, the Sikhs caused devastation with constant guerilla attacks on the Mughal officials who administered these territories. In Ajmer, a city in Rajasthan, the Marathas carved a large territory for themselves and claimed independence from the Mughal Empire. Also, the Deccan was under constant attacks, which led to the destruction of Mughal forts and only sped up the process of the decline of the empire. The Marathas even reached Delhi and raided it in 1737. When signing a peace treaty in Delhi in early 1738, Muhammad Shah ceded Malwa to the Marathas as one of its conditions.

By 1739, the Mughal Empire was weak enough to have become an attractive target for foreign opportunists. Nader Shah of Persia, drawn by the wealth and weakness of the Mughal Empire, launched an attack and captured Kabul, Ghazni, Lahore, and Sindh. At the Battle of Karnal in the same year, the forces of Muhammad Shah were defeated by the Persians in just three hours. The defeat was a hard blow to the Mughal Empire, as it opened the way to Delhi, which Nader Shah's army looted, depriving it of all its riches. The Battle of Karnal was just the start of the foreign invasions, which would continue to weaken the Mughal Empire and lead to its ultimate demise.

The first victory for the Mughal Empire happened in 1748 when they fought the invading Afghans under the leadership of Ahmad Shah Durrani. The Mughal forces were led by the heir apparent of Muhammad Shah, Ahmad Shah Bahadur, and he commanded 75,000 men. The Afghans, who numbered only 12,000, were easily defeated at the Battle of Manupur, and the Mughal Empire celebrated the long-needed victory for days.

The victory at the Battle of Manupur was paid with a heavy price, though. Many died, and the empire's army, although victorious, was devastated. Initially, the numbers of the dead were kept a secret, but once Muhammad Shah learned the truth, he closed himself in his quarters for three days. The emperor was so shocked he could not speak. He spent his days crying out loud, mourning his army. On

April 16th, 1748, Muhammad Shah was found dead in his rooms, and it is recorded that he died of grief.

Chapter 7 – The Final Generations of the Mughals (1748–1857)

Ahmad Shah Bahadur was the son of the previous Mughal emperor, Muhammad Shah, and he to witnessed the decentralization of his father's empire, the conflicts with Maratha, and the invasion from the Persian ruler Nader Shah. Even though Ahmad Shah was the heir apparent, he was constantly belittled by his father, who never even gave him any education, military training, or an allowance worthy of a prince. By the time of his succession, Ahmad Shah Bahadur didn't know how to read or write and was a frequent visitor of the harem. During his rule, the empire was managed by his mother, Qudsia Begum, who entrusted state affairs to the head eunuch of the court.

Once Ahmad Shah was crowned on April 18th, 1748, in the Red Court, he was free from his father's bullying, and he could indulge in his passion for women without anyone stopping him. His love for the harem proved to be no more than a nuisance for his mother, who was given a mansab of 50,000. Under her influence, Ahmad Shah appointed Safdar Jang as the grand vizier, as he was the only able administrator, which he proved by governing Oudh and Kashmir.

Qudsia Begum also influenced the promotion of Javed Khan to the official title of Nawab Bahadur, or chief eunuch. Javed Khan had started as a harem eunuch and eventually progressed to the position of head eunuch of the royal household. It is speculated that because of his youthfulness, robust personality, and handsomeness, Qudsia Begum took him as a lover and had him promoted to become the regent of the Mughal Empire. Just as the Sayyid brothers took control of the many Mughal emperors, so, too, did Ahmad Shah's mother and Javed Khan.

Under the rule of Ahmad Shah Bahadur, the fragmentation of the Mughal Empire continued. The constant internal struggles for power between his regent Javed Khan and his opposition, led by Grand Vizier Safdar Jang, created the fertile ground for the further expansion of the Maratha Confederacy, which, in 1752, imposed a unilateral protectorate over the Mughal court in Delhi. Angered, Ahmad and his court had to retaliate, and in 1754, he launched an attack. The main battle was fought at Sikandarabad, which the Mughals lost, and their imperial household was humiliated. The Mughal emperor fled the battlefield, leaving his mother, wives, and 8,000 women to be captured by Feroze Jung III, better known as Imad-ul-Mulk, a Mughal military commander who had defected and joined the Marathas. Then, Imad-ul-Mulk proceeded to Delhi, where he killed Javed Khan and imprisoned and blinded Emperor Ahmad Shah Bahadur. He was proclaimed as the grand vizier of the Mughal Empire, and he decided to release Prince Aziz-ud-Din from the slums of the Salatin and overthrow Ahmad. The destiny of Qudsia Begum is unknown, but Ahmad Shah was allowed to live until his natural death in 1775. Thrown in the Salatin, he was too poor and wretched to live past the age of 49.

Aziz-ud-Din is better known by his regnal name of Alamgir II. He was the second son of Jahandar Shah, and he ruled the remnants of the Mughal Empire from 1754 until 1759. At the time of his succession, Alamgir was already an old man, as he was almost 55, and he had no administrative or military experience. He was yet another perfect puppet emperor of the too-powerful Mughal courtiers and their families. Imad-ul-Mulk conspired with the Maratha Confederacy, which grew stronger with each passing year. During the reign of Alamgir II and Grand Vizier Imad-ul-Mulk, the Marathas were at the peak of their expansion, which came at the cost of an already weak Mughal Empire.

In the effort to escape the influence of Imad-ul-Mulk, Alamgir II made an alliance with the Durrani Empire (today's territories of Afghanistan and Pakistan) in 1755 and their leader, Ahmad Shah Durrani, who was in Lahore at the time. The Durrani shah and his forces marched to Delhi to get rid of Imad-ul-Mulk and his Maratha allies. Upon arriving, the royal family of Alamgir II met the Durrani leaders, and to strengthen the pact against the Mughal grand vizier, Ahmad's son, Timur Shah Durrani, was engaged to Alamgir's daughter, Zuhra Begum. Ahmad retreated to Kabul, leaving his forces under his son's charge.

However, the Marathas rejected the alliance between the Mughal emperor and the Durrani Empire, and in 1757, they began the siege of Delhi. They made a camp thirty kilometers (almost 19 miles) away from the Red Fort and occupied the surrounding villages, which provided for the Maratha army. The Mughals had only 2,500 soldiers garrisoned inside Delhi, but by positioning heavy artillery on the walls, they were able to resist the attacks for the next five months. However, the help of the Durrani never came, as Ahmad Shah Durrani was too busy fighting resistance in his own empire. After the Marathas managed to cut off the food supply to the city of Delhi, its commander, Naib-ul-Daula, eventually had to surrender and proclaim defeat.

When the Marathas entered the city, they expected to capture the emperor and his royal family, but somehow, Alamgir managed to escape, and he was received as a royal refuge in the Hindu Kingdom of Bharatpur. With the help of Suraj Mal, the ruler of Bharatpur, Alamgir II returned to Delhi with his royal family. Imad-ul-Mulk conspired to assassinate Alamgir II and his whole family, but word of his plans reached the prince and heir, Ali Gohar, who managed to escape. However, he did not save his father; whether this was by choice is not known. Alamgir II was killed in late November 1759, and Imad-ul-Mulk was free to choose the new emperor who would become his puppet. For that role, he chose Shah Jahan III, who ruled for only one year before he was deposed by the Marathas.

The next and sixteenth emperor of the Mughals was Ali Gohar, better known as Shah Alam II, who ruled from 1760 until 1788. As mentioned above, he was the son of Alamgir II and managed to escape Delhi when the plot to assassinate his father became evident to him. He was chosen as the emperor of the Mughal Empire by Ahmad Shah Durrani, who helped him defeat Imad-ul-Mulk and his Maratha allies. However, the Mughal Empire was now reduced to Delhi and the small surrounding areas around the city. The Persians had a saying, "Sultanat-e Shah Alam, Az Dilli ta Palam," which means "The empire of Shah Alam is from Delhi to Palam." Palam remains a suburb of Delhi to this day.

However, Shah Alam wouldn't let his empire to be reduced to only one city. Immediately after succeeding the throne, he tried to restore his authority over Bihar and Bengal. He ordered the submission of the governor of Bengal, who was no more than the puppet figure for the British East India Company. The Company wouldn't surrender its interests to a weak Mughal emperor, and since they owned a private British army, they resisted Alam's advances. Shah Alam invaded Bihar on three occasions, but his army of 30,000 soldiers was no match for the rich British commanders who were determined to stay.

The Mughals were used to Europeans by now as they had fought with or against the Portuguese, who came to these parts of the world as traders. The French followed the Portuguese as the demand for Indian goods grew throughout Europe. The British were the last to come; however, their tactics were significantly different from their European predecessors. The British East India Company never hid the fact that they wanted to get involved in the politics of the Indian subcontinent. Not that the French and Portuguese did not get involved, but they always came with trade as the main reason for their presence in these regions.

During much of the 16th and 17th centuries, trade was indeed the main focus of the East India Company. However, with the decline of the Mughal Empire, their focus shifted to owning its territory. Bengal came under British rule during the Carnatic Wars, which lasted from 1746 to 1763. When the British commanders defeated the Nawabs of Bengal in the Battle of Buxar in 1764, the Company was in full control of the Bengal territory and had all the rights to collect its revenue. The East India Company thus became a major political power in the Indian subcontinent. It had either direct control over the territories it ruled or had it through puppet rulers and governors who were under constant military pressure from the British.

The Company's army wasn't composed of actual British soldiers for the most part. In fact, they hired Indian infantrymen, who were then trained in the European style of warfare. They were called sepoys. Sepoys were always commanded by Europeans, who brought technologically advanced artillery with them, allowing them to easily triumph over the much larger Mughal army.

Once Shah Alam II submitted himself to the East India Company in 1763, the British had even more legitimacy to the rule of the Indian subcontinent. However, Shah Alam wasn't happy with the situation; although he was a weak ruler, he constantly strived for the greatness of his much earlier predecessors. By 1764, he had escaped the British and joined his forces with Shuja-ud-Daulah, the Nawab of Oudh, who previously helped him attack Bengal and Bihar. They tried to invade these territories once again, and the losses they suffered at the Battle of Buxar in 1764 and the Battle of Kora in 1765 were devastating. Shah Alam was again forced to accept the Company as his superior, but he did manage to negotiate a settlement. The Company returned the province of Allahabad to the Mughal emperor, and they promised him an annual tribute of 2,600,000 rupees (today, this sum would be around forty million British pounds). In exchange, Shah Alam allowed whomever the East India Company chose to govern Bengal and Bihar. He also appointed the Company as his diwan in these territories. Diwan was a title used for various offices of the states, and to the Company, it brought legal power to collect revenues in Bengal and Bihar, but it would take the Court of Directors of the East India Company another six or seven years to officially accept the title.

Shah Alam wasn't really satisfied with the deal he made with the East India Company in the Treaty of Allahabad, and he sent a mission to England, pleading King George III to install him back on the throne of Hindustan. He promised that the British king's name would be celebrated throughout the Indian subcontinent and that he would be in personal debt to the British ruler if he officially enthroned him in his former capital of Shahjahanabad (Old Delhi). However, the complex negotiations between the East India Company and the British Parliament thwarted the Mughal mission, and the ambassador who was tasked with it was never presented to the king. The Mughal ambassador, I'tisam-ud-Din, returned to Hindustan in 1769, and besides his report to the emperor, he also wrote the first Indian book about Britain, the travel narrative *Shigurf-nama-i-Wilayat*, "Wonder Book of England."

In 1770, the East India Company paid only 18 percent of their promised annual tribute to Shah Alam II, and in 1772, they paid 23 percent. Yet the Mughal emperor had no other choice but to remain under British protection. The reason might be due to his own weakness and inability to claim what was his by right, or it might have been due to the fact that even such a low amount of money was still a much higher income for the emperor than what he received decades before. Also, aside from some minor issues with the reception protocol, the British officials treated the Mughal emperor with much more respect than his previous regents, the Sayyid brothers, Imad-ul-Mulk, and Ahmad Shah Durrani.

However, Shah Alam II continued to dream of restoring his empire. He begged the East India Company to help him retrieve Shahjahanabad, where much of his court and household remained, but they refused. The Mughal emperor then searched for help elsewhere. In 1771, he gave four million rupees to the Marathas to help him gain control of his previous capital. In addition, he promised the revenues of Allahabad and some other imperial cities. However, even though the military campaign was set out, nothing was achieved. Shah Alam struggled for the next three decades to return the lost glory of the Mughal Empire back, but the political scene of northern India was constantly shifting and changing due to foreign influence. The British East India Company had its own war with the French and could care less about the Mughal emperor. As such, the warlords and regional powers constantly changed, and the emperor lost what little control of the administration of his empire he held in his hands.

In 1788, one of the warlords, Ghulam Qadir, forced Shah Alam II to make him the grand vizier. He had the reputation of an insane person as he was constantly in search of Mughal riches, which he estimated to be around 250 million rupees. He ravaged the Mughal palaces located across the empire in search of these riches, and angered that he could not find anything, he blinded the emperor. Ghulam Qadir was brutal to the already elderly Shah Alam, as well as his family. Anyone who tried to help the bleeding emperor was beheaded. It is also recorded that Ghulam Qadir often pulled the emperor's beard to torture him. He made all of the Mughal princesses dance naked in front of him, after which they all jumped in the Yamuna River to drown.

With Ghulam Qadir as the grand vizier, the honor and prestige of the Mughal Empire was at its lowest. Finally, on October 2nd, 1788, Mahadaji Shinde, the Maratha ruler of Gwalior, killed Ghulam Qadir, taking Delhi under his protection. He restored Shah Alam II to the throne, which was now under the direct protection of the Maratha Confederacy. The Marathas ruled northern India for the next fifteen years, with a garrison permanently occupying Delhi. It was their conflict with the British East India Company in 1803 that overthrew their supremacy in the Mughal Empire.

As a result of the conflict, the East India Company conquered Shahjahanabad and its surrounding regions in 1803, but they still recognized Shah Alam II as the sovereign of the Mughal Empire. However, the emperor was forbidden to engage in the politics of his empire, and in turn, he was given a moderate sum of money as a pension. Shah Alam died in 1806, and his son Akbar II (r. 1806–1837) succeeded the Mughal throne. He, too, was confined in the court of Shahjahanabad and had no power to influence the political events of his empire. He was yet another puppet emperor controlled by the East India Company.

Still, the name of the Timurid emperors was respected by all Indians, and the Mughal court remained an attractive destination to many, whether they were Muslim, Hindu, or British. Although he had no political power, Akbar II managed to preserve the cultural life of Delhi, and the arts was the one thing that kept flourishing during the rule of the last three Mughal emperors. Like his predecessor, Akbar II was a poet, and he invested much in the culture of his crumbling empire. In recognition of his sovereignty, the East India Company issued coins with Persian script and his name. However, he was never more than a prisoner of the Company. In 1835, they even took away his title of emperor, and named him "King of Delhi." It was then that the Company stopped issuing the coins with his name and made all script of the coins in English alone.

However, the Company wasn't ready to proclaim themselves the nominal rulers of the northern Indian territories. Instead, they encouraged the Nawab of Oudh and the Nizam of Hyderabad to take the royal titles and be their puppet rulers. This would further diminish the influence Akbar II still had as the emperor of the Mughals.

When Akbar II died in 1837, the Company enthroned his eldest son, Bahadur Shah II, as their puppet ruler. He was already 62 at the time, and he was happy to stay out of the political life of the empire. In 1850, the British decided that Bahadur Shah would be the last emperor of the Mughals. Their plan was to give the title of prince to Bahadur's heir and force the royal family to retire to a rural retreat that had been specially made for them. However, a massive uprising happened in India in 1857, and Bahadur Shah, even though he was 82, found himself in the middle of current political events.

In May 1857, unsatisfied by the British Christian rule, the Indian sepoys, rulers, and landholders, both Muslim and Hindu, revolted. The old peoples of northern India resented the intrusive lifestyle of the British newcomers, who imposed new social reforms, taxes, and harsh treatment of the natives. They wanted to restore the old Mughal Empire, and the main force of the rebelling army was concentrated around Bahadur Shah II, who the rebels proclaimed as their emperor. The rebels were successful in driving the British out of Shahjahanabad and much of northern India. However, after four months of bloody fighting, the British Army and the Indians who still obeyed them managed to recapture the main city and imprison the last Mughal emperor. After killing all of his sons, the British officers put the old emperor on trial for treason against the East India Company.

The life of emperor Bahadur Shah II was spared, but he and his whole family were exiled to Burma, where he died in 1862. The British rule of the Shahjahanabad destroyed many of the Mughal cultural monuments, as the military officers needed the area around the Red Fort cleared so the artillery on the walls would have a clear view. The Company also desecrated many of the Muslim and Hindu praying sites by celebrating Christian services in them. One of the famous mosques of the city, Jami' Mosque, was entirely destroyed.

Chapter 8 – Memory of the Mughal Empire

The Common People

The world of the Mughal Empire was a world of duality. Where the small number of elite nobles lived their lives preoccupied with wars and court intrigues, the common people of the Indian subcontinent worked to provide for both themselves and the elite. The emperor, his family, and the nobles were rich, and they enjoyed a life filled with art, music, and literature, but the common people of India were illiterate, exhausted, and often starving. While the court life of the Mughal nobles seemed unreachable, it was very much real. However, the greater reality was the barren life of the commoners.

The life of an average Indian in the Mughal Empire advanced little from the conditions in which their predecessors lived a thousand or more years earlier. The houses for the commoners were usually one-room hovels, with the floor made out of beaten earth covered in cow dung. Walls were made out of mud and the roof out of straw. The hovels were just high enough for a man to walk in bent at the waist. The hovels had no windows or doors, just one small opening that served as the entrance and exit. Usually, the commoner would share this hovel with his whole family and livestock if he had any.

Many European travelers were shocked by the duality of the Indian world. While emperors and nobles built grand palaces and temples out of various types of stones and bricks, the common people lived in small decrepit huts built of mud and wood. They had no need for more, for unlike emperors and nobles, the common people spent their days working in the fields, with their livestock, or crafting goods. The women cooked outside, and the children played outside. The inside of the hovels was more protection from the weather, night, and wild beasts, and nothing more. The Europeans often compared these huts to the cells of the prisons of Europe. However, in India, they were the reality of everyday life.

It should be noted that India did have a middle class during the Mughal Empire. Though their numbers were low, and they could hardly be noticed among the masses of poor commoners, the middle class did exist, and they had a better quality of life. While the commoners slept on the floor, which was often muddy, the middle class slept in makeshift hammocks. Due to the constant heat of India, they rarely used any blankets. Their houses, even though they were larger and better, had no tables or chairs; everyone sat on the ground. No one could afford tablecloths or even plates, and both commoners and the middle class used fig leaves to eat from. The same leaves were used as bed sheets or other linen. Even liquid could be held in the leaves, which were joint in such a masterful way that there was no leakage. Pots and other kitchen utensils were mostly made out of earthenware, and only a few of the middle class could afford a copper drinking cup.

What shocked the Christian Europeans the most was the way Indians, both Muslim and Hindu, dressed. The poorest of the commoners, both men and women, had only a piece of cloth tied to their waistline, which was big enough to cover their private parts. Women would sometimes cover their heads if they had extra material from their waistcloth. Since Europeans and the founder of the Mughal Empire, Babur, described Indian clothing the same way, it would appear that nothing changed in over two centuries. The Jesuits were especially shocked that Indians thought it was normal to pray to their gods half-naked. Only the soldiers had a bit more clothing, as well as a cloth tied around their heads. Laborers, commoners, and some soldiers had an extra piece of cloth that would serve them as a garment during the day and as bed linen during the night. This way, they were ready to sleep wherever they found themselves. It was usually the people of the middle class who could afford to wear a short shirt; sometimes, it would even be made of silk. However, no one except the nobles could afford shoes.

In the regions of India that are known for colder climates, the people wore more clothes. In Kashmir, it was common for both men and women to wear woolen tunics, and in the regions of Varanasi, the people were described wearing silk dhotis and scarfs. How people dressed was greatly determined by the region where they lived and its climate. What common people saved on clothing, they spent on ornaments and jewelry. European travelers through the Mughal Empire describe that families would rather die of hunger than have no ornaments to show off. Men also used their hairs as a type of ornament, especially Hindus, who wore it long and tied it to the side of their head. Muslims, especially Shia Muslims, shaved their heads. They also preferred beards, while the Hindus usually had only mustaches.

Just like their huts and their clothing, the food of the commoners was very poor. In the Mughal Empire, most Hindus were not vegetarians, but hardly anyone could afford meat. Usually, their meals would be grain-based, often with added greens, and mixed with rice. Indians had one big meal a day, usually at midday. The dish was rice-based, and the coastal people would often have a piece of dried fish as well. The meat from goats, chickens, or sheep was reserved for the nobles, and the commoners would eat it only during festivities. Europeans describe beef as being the cheapest meat in India, but no Hindu would eat it, as the cow was their sacred animal. However, Muslims were allowed to eat beef, although they regarded beef as lesser. Emperors Akbar and Jahangir prohibited the slaughter of cows, and during their reigns, beef wasn't available to anyone. Furthermore, the peacock was a sacred bird, and shellfish was considered impure by both Muslims and Hindus. Pig meat was a taboo for the Muslims, but Hindus ate it if they could afford it. It was usually served to the Hindu nobles, though. However, hunting wasn't prohibited for the common people, and if they could catch a wild animal, they would eat it. Wheat was too expensive for the commoners, so they did not make bread out of it. Their main protein and other nutrients sources were from legumes, millets, and rice.

Although cows were sacred to Hindus, that doesn't mean they weren't useful. They still provided milk, and the people would use raw milk in their food or make butter and ghee out of it. However, milk wasn't the only product from cows that they would drink. In Mughal India, it was considered a sacred thing to drink a cow's urine. People would scoop the urine with their hands and take a sip, then wash their faces with the rest of it. By doing so, they would be able to proclaim themselves as cleansed and holy.

Although both Muslim and Hindu citizens of the Mughal Empire had their own taboos and generally didn't indulge in vices, both societies were very open toward sex. European travelers were shocked to learn that Indians didn't bother to hide when they consummated their marriages. The upper-class men basically had the right to take whichever woman they wanted, even if she was married to someone else. Muslim women were kept pure, but they, too, would secretly indulge in romantic relationships outside of their marriage. Muslim men, on the other hand, were allowed just about anything. They would often use children as old as seven or eight, and among nobles, homosexuality was normal. Hindus regarded homosexuality as wrong as eating beef, and it was unheard of in their society, although incest would happen, albeit very rarely, and even then, it would be punished.

Prostitution, on the other hand, was a very common thing in India, although each emperor had his own opinion on it. While Akbar set up a camp for the prostitutes and ordered all of their customers to be recorded, Emperor Shah Jahan allowed them everywhere and was even a frequent guest of the brothels. Hijras, the hermaphrodites for which India is known for even today, were very common during the Mughal period, and the Jesuits would beg the Mughal emperors to ban them, for which they were often laughed at.

Harems and the Position of Women

In Arabic, harem means a sacred, prohibited space. It was a common practice to include a harem in the courts of the Mughal Empire, and it was there that the women of the household lived. Their world was essentially vacuum-sealed and private, but harems were not exclusive to the imperial palaces. Households of notable nobles and state officials, both Muslim and Hindu, had their own harems. Traditionally, in India, women were not secluded or veiled until the Rajputs adopted the practice by imitating their Muslim superiors. Even then, purdah, the practice of veiling women to hide them from the sight of strangers, was not enforced on women; it was more of a status symbol for wealthy families. In some areas of the Mughal Empire, even Muslim women didn't veil themselves, for example, in the Deccan sultanates. In the territories of Kerala, women were not just free to do whatever they wanted, but they also held immense power, just like the men did.

Among the poor, there was no seclusion for the women. Since life was so basic, they couldn't allow for the dividing of men from women. Female Hindu and Muslim commoners had to work and earn their own living, and the hot climate of India prevented working men and women from wearing more clothes than necessary to cover their private parts. However, the ruling class was divided into two separate worlds, one of the men and the other of women. The women from rich and powerful families were often confined in their apartments and mansions. They were guarded jealously and were burned alive when the man of the house died, though this practice was mainly tied to Hindu culture.

For the ruling class, women were property, although a very valuable one. For a noblewoman, known as a begum, such life was desired above all, as they were treated well and often with respect.

Even though they were property, women observed their seclusion as a privilege, not a punishment. In rare moments, they were allowed outside of the palaces and mansions, although the noble women of Muslim culture had to wear a burka, a loose garment that would cover their whole body, even the head. If they traveled to accompany their men, women were carried in covered litters, and no one was allowed to set eyes on them. Emperors never allowed a building to be built anywhere near the harem so that the sacred place could not be looked at. In fact, the jealousy of the Mughals went so far that husbands wouldn't allow their fathers-in-law or brothers-in-law to speak with their daughters and sisters unless they were present.

If a begum allowed herself to be seen in public, it meant either divorce or death. Divorce was no better as it almost certainly meant death, for her own family would denounce her. Even if she accidentally revealed herself, death was the only honorable way out for her. However, looking at royal women was not the only taboo in the world of the Mughal Empire. To speak a royal woman's name was also considered to be forbidden. To the outside world, these women were nameless, and women considered that to be the highest honor. Still, begums did exist, and in order to refer to them, people had to come up with beautiful epithets that would substitute their true names.

It is wrongly presumed that the imperial harem of the Mughal emperors was only reserved for his wives and concubines. In fact, the harem was a place where all the women of the household lived, which included queens, mothers, sisters, and closer or distant relatives. The harem had its guards, administrators, cooks, and servants, and the emperor would appoint his favorite begum as the head of the harem. Aside from the lavish life provided by the palace, each begum would receive her salary, and in the Mughal world, the amount of money they received varied based on their position and value to the emperor. It could be anywhere between 3 to 1,600 rupees a month. Some women received more money than a Mughal soldier would. With their money, begums were able to build tombs, temples, and other monuments in the glory of the empire. Some women were great patrons of art, while others cherished education.

Another wrong belief is that Mughal emperors had thousands of women in their harems who were there just for their satisfaction. Although the harems were vast and many women lived there, the emperors were simply people with the same needs just like any other men. They could not possibly waste their days in the harem, and they usually had only one favorite wife they would often go to. The harem was a symbol of power in the Mughal Empire, and that is why they were so large. Polygamy also wasn't just an excuse for pleasure. The emperor could have multiple wives for political reasons or as a favor to his best officers. Royal marriages were often enforced by peace treaties or alliances. Polygamy also occurred to ensure many children and, most importantly, to produce an heir to the Mughal throne. In that period of history, especially in Hindustan, children were often lost due to diseases that had no cures, or they would be killed in one of the many wars.

The emperors spent most of their days inside the harem, but it is wrong to believe that it was for pleasure. In fact, the emperor's offices were in the harem, and many women who lived there held their own offices, which were sometimes even equivalent to the office in the outside world. Women of the harem were educated, and they were the ones who did the administrative work of the empire. The harem is where emperors did their most confidential work, and they would often rely on the women to help. Women of the harem were often included in the business of the government, especially if the business was a family matter. The begums were allowed to attend meetings, although behind walls, curtains, or screens, so that they would be familiar with the matters of the state. These women often used their wits and cunning to manage the empire alongside the emperors. And often, they used their influence to steer politics the way they wanted. There was no better place to persuade the emperor than in the confined apartments of the harem.

The rich life of a begum provided the royal women with everything they wanted and more. However, they were greatly deprived of life, or at least that's how modern readers would see it. Mughal princesses didn't marry, as Emperor Akbar proclaimed that no man was worthy of a Mughal woman. Confined in their golden cage, the Mughal royal women had no family. They were basically taken away from their parents and locked away, never to see their brothers and sisters again. Only the privileged wives had children, and even those children were often taken away to be brought up in other parts of the empire. All the luxuries they enjoyed could not compensate for the loneliness they must have felt. To fill their days, many women occupied themselves with arts and crafts, such as embroidery, stitching, painting, and writing. Music and dancing were allowed as well in the harem, but some of the emperors would frown upon it, as the Muslim culture was against it.

The begums were the silent and invisible power that ran politics from behind the throne. Royal women wielded great power, and as such, they influenced events. It is no wonder they saw their place in the harem as prestigious and not as a punishment or form of bondage. Muslims denied women from playing a public role, but from the harem, a woman could have as much power as the emperor himself. However, being away from the public eye meant many of the great women of the Mughal Empire remain unknown to history. Although some were so exceptional that their names were recorded and remembered, most of them are lost to the past. The most remarkable of the Mughal queens is certainly Nur Jahan, the wife of Emperor Jahangir. She was even recognized as the real force behind the throne while her husband indulged in opium. She is the first and only queen of the Mughal Empire that has coins issued in her own name.

Culture

Illustration by the 17th-century Mughal artist Ustad Mansur
https://upload.wikimedia.org/wikipedia/commons/thumb
/d/d3/Mansur-8.png/800px-Mansur-8.png

Culture flourished during the 16th and 17th centuries when the Mughals were at the height of their power in northern India. As patrons of many arts, it is no wonder the Mughal period is one of the most fruitful when it comes to culture. Not only did the Muslim culture enjoy the patronage of the Mughal emperors, but so did the Hindus. It is during this period that Hindu poetry, and literature in general, came to its heights.

Although Muslim and Hindu cultures coexisted in the Mughal Empire for a very long time, they influenced each other very little. Any influence that did happen was only superficial. This was due to the serious social segregation between the ruling Muslims and the subjected Hindus. While the Muslims observed Hindu culture as less important and not worthy of their attention, Hindus did not allow the Muslim way of life to influence their conservative society. Instead, they shaped their culture around Islam, being careful not to mix the two.

The Mughals generally came from a very abundant cultural background, and they enjoyed the intellectual and artistic achievements of their people. After all, they came from Central Asia, a territory that is known for mixing the cultures of three of the great civilizations of classic times, India, China, and Greece. Growing up with such traditions, the Mughal emperors themselves were multi-talented. Some of them are even known for their great cultural achievements. Babur, the founder of the Mughal Empire, was an accomplished author, composer, and calligrapher. Humayun was a lover of natural sciences and a great mathematician, astronomer, poet, and inventor. Akbar was a philosopher with a different set of skills, which included poetry, architecture, and music. Aurangzeb was the only Mughal emperor who didn't appreciate culture and had no skills of his own. But, as if to compensate for her father's inability in the field of arts, his daughter, Zeb-un-Nissa, was an avid patron of all kinds of arts and education.

The reign of Emperor Akbar was the most exciting time for culture, mainly in the field of science. Akbar and his subjects had a habit of looking toward the future of the empire, and for this, they were mocked by the traditionalists who found comfort in the past. But it was during his reign that science prospered, as people with ideas were valued above all. Natural sciences and medicine were very popular fields, and the emperor himself was very interested in the European discoveries in these disciplines. Although Akbar invested in bringing European technologies to the empire, mainly into the Mughal military, the people of India were generally not interested in anything European. Thus, the emperor couldn't instill the values of European sciences and crafts to his people. The best his people could do was mimic foreign products, which led to low-quality items. Indians never showed much interest in learning European technology and applying that knowledge to advance their own culture.

As patrons of the arts, the emperors expected artists to please them. This is why it was very hard for Mughal artists to express themselves or develop new techniques. All they could do was what their masters and employers wanted. They could not risk displeasing the nobles as they would risk not just their wellbeing but also their lives. An angry emperor could always order an artist to be executed. It was the same for the practitioners of medicine. If they were unable to cure a prominent officer or even emperor, they faced the prohibition of their practice or even execution.

Literature was highly valued in the Mughal Empire, and it was never really censored. Even when it portrayed a noble or a ruler in a bad light, the authors were never punished. Satire in literature was observed as a commentary on the events and persons, and it would often be taken as such. However, neither Muslim nor Hindu authors practiced mocking the rulers openly. Books and scripts were treated as treasures, and whenever a city was conquered, the libraries were treated with the utmost respect. Even though entire cities were burned as a display of power, the Mughal emperors would first loot them, and the books were a part of that loot, safely packed for transportation to the royal library. Even prominent women of the harem had their own libraries, and ladies, such as Jahanara and Zeb-un-Nissa, had some of the richest libraries of the Mughal Empire.

Poetry was so popular that the nobles often exchanged letters written in verse. When challenging another to a duel, one would write it down in verse, and the reply would also be in the form of poetry. Even though Emperor Akbar was illiterate or dyslexic, he kept a library that contained over 24,000 volumes. He employed people to read to him, and not just official letters and documents but books and poetry as well.

However, the most prominent artistic achievements of the Mughal Empire lay in its architecture, although the Mughals did not contribute much to the originality of the architecture but to its refinement instead. Their buildings were inspired by the Persian culture. They weren't even the first to introduce the Persian style into the architecture of India as the Delhi Sultanate did it before the Mughals. However, what is special about Mughal architecture is the degree of its refinement. Even today, Mughal buildings and monuments belong in another class by themselves.

Landscaping and gardening were other passions of the Mughal emperors, and even though the principle of public parks and gardens was known to India before the Mughals, they were the ones who extensively refined it. The gardens were a great love of the Mughals, and wherever they chose to stop, usually for weeks or months at a time, a garden had to be erected. The Mughals also introduced new plant and animal species into the Indian world, first from their native Central Asia and later on from Europe and the Americas. The gardens were places of relaxation and contemplation, a delightful piece of heaven on the ruthless and hot earth. The Mughal gardens were square or rectangular in their base and were divided into partitions, always using straight lines, never curves. They would create a grid, as in a network of passages, and in between them, they would landscape. The water was often directed through the garden, and it would freshen up the pleasant air, which was already rich with oxygen and exotic scents of various plants.

The nobles lived in vast, open buildings, and they cherished the open view, so no large trees were planted outside the palaces and mansions. While Hindu architecture reflected the conservative hidden lifestyle of its people, Mughal buildings were huge, cheerful, and reflected the adventurous lives of the Central Asians. They were richly decorated with paintings and stone carvings. The Mughals loved arches and latticed windows, which were always open, allowing the daylight and night breeze to play in the vast hallways and rooms. Unlike the Mughal structures, Hindus built small, dark, and airless rooms in which they felt safely confined.

Akbar was the first emperor who dared to combine the Persian and Indian styles of architecture. He built many buildings, of which the most famous were the Agra Fort and the elegant pavilion bridge across the Gomati River near the city of Jaunpur. Akbar usually chose red sandstone for his buildings, and marble was used only as a decoration, never as a building material. The ornaments of Akbar's buildings were usually low relief stone carvings and paintings on plastered surfaces. It was only with the reign of Shah Jahan that gem inlays became the hallmark of Mughal architecture. Apart from forts and palaces, the emperors built mosques and tombs, which were as rich as any other Mughal building. Gardens were part of every Mughal structure, be it a mansion, palace, mosque, or even a tomb. In fact, tombs of the Mughal royal family were often the centerpieces of a vast garden.

Certainly, the most famous tomb, and a staple of Mughal architecture, is the Taj Mahal, which was built as a resting place for Mumtaz Mahal, the favorite wife of emperor Shah Jahan. However, the Taj Mahal, although beautiful, brought nothing new to Mughal masonry. The inspiration for the most famous tomb was drawn from previous Mughal building achievements, specifically the tombs of Timur, the progenitor of the dynasty, and Humayun's tomb with its gardens.

The Taj Mahal in Agra, India
https://en.wikipedia.org/wiki/Mughal_Empire#/media/
File:Taj_Mahal_(Edited).jpeg

The Taj Mahal is a complex of buildings in a beautiful garden. The tomb is just the central part of this complex, and it is built completely in white marble. Other buildings are mausoleums for Shah Jahan's other wives, a mosque, and a building that may have served as a guesthouse. The garden has its main gate, a monument constructed of marble, and vast pathways with a lake in the middle. The tomb of Mumtaz Mahal and Shah Jahan himself is a symmetrical building with a square base and an arch-shaped doorway. It is topped with a large white dome, and it has four minarets that serve as a frame for the tomb.

Both external and internal decorations of the Taj Mahal are the finest examples of Mughal artistry. The tomb is richly decorated with paintings, stone carvings, and calligraphy. The elements in these are mostly flora or abstract forms, as Islam prohibits anthropomorphic forms. The complex is inscribed with passages from the Quran, which serve both as decoration and as a lesson. The inside of the tomb goes well beyond the traditional decorative elements, as precious and semi-precious stones were used to create masterful works. The interior dome is decorated with the painted sun motif, and it has special openings for light to enter.

Many myths envelop the construction of the Taj Mahal. A story of the twin tombs of the Taj Mahal being built from black stone dates from 17th-century European travelers. Some say how everyone who was involved in the construction of the Taj Mahal had to sign a contract stating that they would not work on a similar design in the future. Others tell stories of how Shah Jahan punished and mutilated the workers and artisans who displeased him. There was even a theory that the Taj Mahal was designed by an Italian or French architect, and others even claim that it was King Parmar Dev of central India who originally built the Taj Mahal in 1196. However, all of these claims are easily disproved as there is written contemporary evidence of its construction.

Some people believe that the Taj Mahal should be enlisted as a new Wonder of the World, and several petitions are going on for the tomb to be recognized as such by state officials. In 1983, the Taj Mahal was designated as a UNESCO World Heritage Site, and it is truly a jewel of the former Mughal Empire. Over 20,000 artisans worked under the supervision of the imperial architect, Ustad Ahmad Lahori, and together, they built a unique monument dedicated to love.

Conclusion

It is as if Aurangzeb, the last strong ruler of the Mughal Empire, saw the end. He wrote letters to his sons just a few days before his death, and in them, he stated that there was no hope for the future. Even though it took much more time for the empire to finally dissolve, after the death of Aurangzeb, the powerful courtiers took his descendants under their control, creating the puppet emperors whose only role was to sit on the throne and pass their days investing in arts and entertainment.

However, it is astonishing to think about how the Mughal dynasty inspired awe and admiration in the people of India. Even when their time was up, and their power was almost non-existent, no one dared to take the empire in their own name. There always had to be a Mughal on the throne. They started as unwanted newcomers, foreigners who conquered a distant land. However, they became an ever-needed presence, without whose name the land would crumble.

Even the Europeans did not dare to officially dethrone the Mughal emperor. They had to create a different narrative for the diverse peoples of India in order to persuade them to give up on their traditions. Eventually, the British East India Company took charge and removed the feeble old Mughal emperor, who did nothing notable except enjoy poetry and music. Like a criminal, he was arrested, quickly tried, and then exiled. The empire was no more.

However, there is a hollow prestige of the word Mughal that remains. It is still associated with the rich and exotic cultures of a distant past. And it is not the memory of the Mughals that haunt us today and draw us closer to their world. It is all of the monuments, buildings, music, calligraphy, history, scripts, and biographies of those emperors that still survive. Whether one looks at the Hindustani language, the *Baburnama* and *Akbarnama*, the glorious gardens of India, the Red Fort, the Taj Mahal, or all the other cultural heritage sites that the Mughals left behind, one thing remains clear. They all stand witness to the power and greatness of one of the richest empires in history.

References

Avasthy, R. S. (1967). *The Mughal Emperor Humayun*. Allahabad: History Dept., University of Allahabad.

Losty, J. P., & Roy, M. (2012). *Mughal India: Art, Culture and Empire: Manuscripts and Paintings in the British Library*. London: The British Library.

Ojha, P. N. (1979). *Glimpses of Social life in Mughal India*. New Delhi: Classical Publications.

Richards, J. (1996). *The Mughal Empire*. Cambridge: Cambridge University Press.

Sarkar, J. (1932). *Fall of the Mughal Empire*. Calcutta: M.C. Sarkar.

Sezgin, F., 'Amāwī Māzin, Ehrig-Eggert, C., & Neubauer, E. (1997). *Mughal India according to European travel accounts: texts and studies*. Frankfurt am Main: Institute for the History of Arabic-Islamic Science.

Shashi, S. S. (1999). *Babar: The First Mughal Emperor of India*. New Delhi: Anmol Publications.

Here's another book by Captivating History
that you might be interested in